MW00710550

look at a
single woman's
daily battles
& blessings

Living Single

One Day at a Time

Liz!
The Lord is
our refuge + strength —
He is so faithful!
Love
Wilda

An honest
look at the
single woman's
daily battles
& blessings

Living Single
One Day at a Time

Jane Wilder

TATE PUBLISHING & Enterprises

Tate Publishing
& Enterprises

Living Single One Day at a Time
Copyright © 2006 by Jane Wilder. All rights reserved.

No part of this publication may be reproduced, stored in a retrieval system or transmitted in any way by any means, electronic, mechanical, photocopy, recording or otherwise without the prior permission of the author except as provided by USA copyright law.

Unless otherwise noted, scripture quotations are taken from the Holy Bible, New International Version ®, Copyright © 1973, 1978, 1984 by International Bible Society. Used by permission of Zondervan Publishing House. All rights reserved.

Scripture quotations marked "NAS" are taken from the New American Standard Bible ®, Copyright © 1960, 1962, 1963, 1968, 1971, 1972, 1973, 1975, 1977, 1995 by The Lockman Foundation. Used by permission. All rights reserved.

In some instances, names have been changed to protect the identity of the persons involved.

Book design copyright © 2006 by Tate Publishing, LLC. All rights reserved.
Cover design by Janae Glass
Interior design by Brandon Wood

Published in the United States of America

ISBN: 15988650–7-2
06.10.30

Dedicated to my many former roommates and current friends with whom living single has been a less lonely existence.

Dedicated to my parents, Bill and Barbara Wilder, who taught me to live life honestly and responsibly—thank you for being my protectors and providers.

Acknowledgments

I am thankful to Julie Lucaci. God used her mightily to inspire and prod me to finish writing this book. Thanks, Julie, for giving me much needed feedback and encouragement.

I am thankful to Dena Owens for her keen eye and attention to detail as she assisted in the editing process.

I am thankful to the many single women who shared stories of their struggles and God's faithful provisions.

I am so grateful to God for prompting me by his Holy Spirit to tackle things in life I would never imagine doing of my own accord.

Table
of
Contents

Introduction

I still remember my first "crush." Well, more accurately, crushes, because they were twins. I was 12 years old and in the sixth grade and Larry and Terry Thomas were in my thoughts more often than I would care to admit. I secretly hoped that they would notice me—a shy, glasses-wearing, braces-bearing, acne-infested, greasy-haired girl. But they did not notice. Chuck, a short blond-haired kid, liked me, but I didn't care—I wanted the Thomas twins. Why was I so head-over-heels for those two twins? Was it their godly personalities? Was it their gentlemanly ways? Was it their drive for success? I hate to say it, but my crush was based solely on their hip looks and classroom charisma. It is dumbfounding what feathered brown hair and wide-legged blue jeans will do to a 12-year-old girl!

I fondly recall Chachi's first appearance on the 70's sit-com, *Happy Days*. I was in love with him, but, alas, he was in love with Joanie. As I watched from TV land while he wooed Joanie, a spark of romance ignited in my preteen heart. Consequently, throughout junior high and high school, I became a girl who craved a boyfriend more than most other things in life. I believed deeply that he would meet my every need and want. He alone would help me feel pretty, loved, and important. I longed to feel my heart pound when he would walk my way. I longed to experience chills as he grabbed my hand. My hope was in that special someone. Although I was a believer from a very young age, I did not understand the concept that God could be sufficient for me.

From that first crush on the Thomas twins, I always assumed I would someday find my prince charming, get married, have kids and enjoy an incredibly perfect life. It never entered my mind that I might be single at 39 and that those dreams might never become a reality.

At the tender age of twelve, I began a life-long search for the love of my life. And that search continues to this day. In some ways the quest is different now than it was back then. I know more of God and am allowing him to work through me in my single state. But the desire to be married has not waned. I still hold on to the hope of finding a life partner who will be my best friend and will have the same passion to serve Christ that I do.

This book is not about a woman who is perfectly content in her singleness. This book is not about someone who has found complete fullness in Christ alone. This book is not about a person who feels the Lord's sufficiency at all times. This book is not about a woman who doesn't crave her home to be filled with a male presence. But this book is about a woman who is striving to please the Lord in her singleness. This book is an honest look at the struggles of the single woman and the hope that comes out of the struggles. I pray that by reading this you will be touched to desire Christ more and to look to him to meet your needs, whether you remain single for a short time or for a life time.

Come, walk with me, as I share my journey as a single woman, desiring a man but also knowing a man—Jesus—who has yet to disappoint.

The Calling

1

Is singleness a calling or a choice? Or does singleness just "happen" to certain kinds of people? Single adult Christians have wrestled with these questions from ancient times until the present.

For a long time I felt strongly that the Lord was calling me to be single. How did I know this? Over the course of several years, God knocked on my heart's door and subtlety yet firmly informed me that he wanted me to be single. I did not know then if that meant for a season or for the whole of my life. I will share with you one particular time that the Lord clearly challenged me regarding this sensitive area of my heart.

Several years ago, while in my early 30's, I had an experience with the Lord that I remember to this day. Prior to this encounter with God, I had never heard his voice audibly, but this time was different. In the middle of the night, I lay asleep in bed, when I was awakened by a voice that clearly asked me the question, "Are you willing?" This voice seemed almost audible because it was so loud in my spirit. At that moment, it was obvious that God was trying to get my attention.

I immediately said to the voice, "Am I willing to do what?" All the while I knew in my heart that God was asking me if I was willing to be single. I wish I could tell you that my next response was one of godliness and complete humility. I wish I could say that, like Samuel in the Bible, I quickly said, "Speak, Lord, for your servant is listening" (I Samuel 3:9b). Unfortunately, I responded by covering my head with my blankets while pretending that I had not heard what God had asked of me.

As the sun rose the next morning, beaconing bedbugs and humans toward the start of a new day, I wished the call I had heard the night before was simply a bad dream. I knew in my spirit, however, that I needed to surrender this area of my life to the Lord. So I took a journey out of the city to spend some quiet time with him. As I sat in my car in a forest preserve parking lot, I considered the question I had been asked the night before. I knew that I had to relinquish my will to the Lord in this tender area of my life. So as the tears flowed freely, I surrendered to my Father, the one who knows best. I told the Lord that I would be willing to remain single, even if that meant for a lifetime.

Did I like this call that God made on my life in the middle of the night? NO! But nonetheless, the Lord made it plain and clear that he wanted me single. I did not know whether God was calling me to be single for a short period or for all of my life. Only recently have I felt the freedom from the Lord to think and pray about marriage.

Let's Back Up

Prior to the above experience and "the call," God taught me much through trying times of unfulfilled longings. As I mentioned previously, I had always wanted to get married. But as year after year passed, the dream did not come true.

In high school I didn't date much. I was very shy and very picky. In college, the same held true. I dated a few guys very briefly, even some unbelievers, but the guys I really liked never showed any interest in me. As I graduated from college, turned 22 and watched several friends tie the knot, I feared that time was running out. I began to feel desperate to find my husband yet frightened that I never would.

After what seemed like ages, but was only one year, I began my first relationship with a very godly and talented man named Paul. We "hung out" for four months and then finally made the decision to be exclusive.

What hit me next, though, would become a pattern for me for the next fifteen years of my life. During the first week of our exclusive relationship, I began to feel unsettled and unpeaceful. I battled those feelings for a short time, trying desperately to convince myself that they were simply "new boyfriend jitters." But this just wasn't true. I felt separated from God and disobedient. God was directing me to end the relationship. Therefore, because my relationship with God was more important than my relationship with this man, I broke it off with the unsuspecting gentleman.

That was the most difficult step of obedience I had ever taken in my life. I liked the guy and couldn't fathom that God was asking me to let go—to let go of the dream that I had cherished in my heart for so long.

But as always, God was faithful. Over time he took the pain away and I realized that Paul was probably not the best for me. So when my roommate came to me and let me know she was interested in him, I was okay with it. Yes, they actually did end up getting married. (Don't feel sorry for me—it's fine! I'm over it! Move on!) God showed me through that experience and several like it in the years to come that he is sovereign. He knows what is good and he works constantly for that good purpose to transpire. We must simply work to trust and obey our Master. Philippians 2:12b and 13 says, "… continue to work out your salvation with fear and trembling, for it is God who works in you to will and to act according to his good purpose."

After Paul, I fell for many other men. There was Matthew, Mark, Luke, and John, among others. (Did you notice that the names have been changed?) With each, I did not feel a peace about dating them. It was torture as I began the enjoyable process of getting to know these godly men, only to have to turn away from them out of sheer obedience to God.

Many times I asked God why. I even questioned his love for me as I cried tears of longing with my cat, Emma Petey, staring up at me as if I were crazy. (Okay, sometimes a bitter cry can even be funny when your pet is gazing your way, probably assuming that you have finally lost it!)

In the climax of one of my favorite movies, *Sense and Sensibility*[1], Eleanor, the eldest of three sisters, discovers that her hopes of marriage are dashed. She is shocked to find that Edward, a man with whom she had developed intimacy and friendship, had made a foolish promise of marriage to another woman. He did not love the other woman, but he intended to honor his promise. As she realizes that she will be divided forever from a man she is desperately in love with, Eleanor makes this statement: "Edward made his promise a long time ago, long before he met me. I believe that he will be happy in the knowledge that he did his duty and kept his word." Eleanor was pleased that "her man" had done what was right, even though his strength of character left her with a broken heart.

I found each of the above situations bearable only because I knew I had listened to God and had been obedient to him. Like Eleanor, I found comfort in the knowledge that the right thing had been done. As I have been obedient to the Lord in this area of my love life, I have also had the joy and privilege of growing through the difficulties. I share with you the following five ways that God has used these times of trial.

I Have Known Emotional Pain

Recently, I was on a long flight from Nairobi, Kenya, to London, England, after a two-week mission trip in Africa. God placed me next to a handsome young man named Rob for the duration of the flight. Both of us were bumped up to business class and began talking about how happy we were to be able to stretch out!

As we continued to converse, I discovered he was finishing a Master's degree at Oxford University and was soon headed to Stanford University in California to begin his doctorate. He definitely had book smarts and a love for learning, but I wondered about his soul. Fortunately, it wasn't long before our conversation turned to spiritual matters. As we talked, one thing stuck in my mind. He said he was happy the way he was. He admitted, though, that to this point, he had experienced a relatively "easy" life. He was fairly sure, though, he would still hold to his agnostic beliefs if things got worse.

Let's face it—there is trouble in this life. Although Rob hasn't experienced a lot of trials yet, he undoubtedly will. I pray that when that time comes, the verses that I shared and my challenge to him to read the Bible will ring clear in his mind.

I am so thankful that I have experienced trials in this life—no, not because I am a masochist, but because pain brings opportunities to grow and to glorify the Lord in a very unique way.

The times that I had to let go of those men did bring severe emotional pain. Others who have gone through abuse, death of a loved one, divorce, and other difficulties may discount my pain as trivial. But it has been pain, my pain, and it is, well—pain. I am definitely not trying to get psycho-analytical here, but we need to remember that pain comes in different shapes and sizes. What is painful for one may not be hurtful for another.

One day, about a year ago, the backwash of some boy troubles left me feeling extremely down and out. I called a long lost friend and was dismayed to learn details of her story of hurt, betrayal and abuse in her marriage. When she asked how I was, I felt stupid even mentioning my own broken heart. However, even in the midst of her own stressful situation, she listened to my heart. She freed me up to express my hurt. She compassionately affirmed the pain I was attempting to trivialize.

We are all made differently and God sees our differences and meets us in the midst of that thing with which we are struggling. I am not writing this to give you an excuse to whine about your pain, but to give you the freedom to go to God and ask for his help and comfort no matter how trivial the trial may appear to you or someone else.

God cared when I was hurting. Some of you are in a fierce battle to let someone go who is not God's best. God sees your fight. Wait, he doesn't just see it, he gets in the ring with you. The Olympic boxer has a boxing coach for a reason. He pays him big bucks to gain wisdom and expertise on how to win the big fight. The coach also trains the boxer toward top physical condition for the day of the fight. But no coach gets in the ring with his boxer. On the day of the fight, the boxer must fight his own battle. On your day of battle, however, God fights with you as you use his weapons of warfare. He gives you victory as you seek to be obedient!

Perhaps you are not getting attention from any man at this time and you are feeling alone and undesirable. God also craves to meet you in the midst of the struggle, to open your eyes that you might find hope in your identity in Christ. He desires to give you a great hope and a future! First Peter 5:6–7 brings clarity as we attempt to comprehend how peace can prevail in the midst of trouble. "Humble yourselves, therefore, under God's mighty hand, that he may lift you up in due time. Cast all your anxiety on him because he cares for you." God desires to meet you in your despairing and fearful moments. Of course, this requires you to surrender to his will, but what a great result—being lifted up by the mighty hand of God! Can you just picture God's strong arm reaching down from heaven to strengthen you and even bring about good in your time of trial?

Just a moment ago, I mentioned finding your identity in Christ. I think we could all benefit from a little segue down Identity in Christ Lane. Let's stop and recall who we are in Jesus:

1. I Peter 2:9–10–A chosen people, a royal priesthood, a people belonging to God: Hey snap out of it! You're God's child. You've been chosen by Him. He is your perfectly wise Father. You have a heavenly inheritance. Thank him for what he has freely given you!
2. I Thessalonians 5:4–5–Sons of the light and of the day: We don't have to cringe in a dark corner, afraid of what trials or even what God will do to us. We can walk in truth, in freedom, and in honesty.
3. I Corinthians 12:27–The body of Christ: "Now you are the body of Christ, and each one of you is a part of it." We have purpose. We have reason for living. We are called to serve as part of the body of Christ.
4. Matthew 5:13–The salt of the earth: You have some important information to share with others, girlfriend!
5. Matthew 5:14–The light of the world: A light will illuminate even in the blackest of rooms. Burn brightly, baby!
6. Ephesians 2:10–God's workmanship, created in Christ Jesus to do good works

7. Ephesians 2:19–Members of God's household
8. II Corinthians 5:20–Christ's ambassadors
9. Romans 6:18–Set free from sin and slaves to righteousness: We can be set free from the self-focus we are tempted toward in certain sorrowful seasons of singleness.
10. II Corinthians 5:17–A new creation: The other day I was driving in downtown Chicago and I heard this kid singing at the top of his lungs from the window of a school bus, "You're beautiful! You're beautiful, it's true!" by James Blunt.[2] I pretended for a moment that it was me he was crooning. But then I looked up and noticed about a million gorgeous, yuppie-type women crossing the street in front of the bus. I don't think it was me he was serenading! Others may not notice us, but the fact is that God has made us beautiful Christ-like creatures. Weird Al Yankovic would like to tell us another story with his parody entitled *You're Pitiful*.[3] Here are a few lines from the song. "My life is brilliant. Your life's a joke. You're just pathetic. You're always broke. And ya smell repulsive too. What a bummer bein' you." That is what our snakey, sinister, enemy is trying to tell you. Don't listen. Turn that song off! You're beautiful, baby! (disclaimer: I don't know what you look like on the outside, I'm talking about your Christ-like qualities flowing from the inside out. I can say this because I am definitely no Cindy Crawford!)

I hope the above verses are encouraging you to stop singing the "I feel sorry for my single self" blues.

Although you no longer need to sing the blues, it is possible that you may be feeling a little blue. In your state of sadness, God desires for you to cry out to him—to trust him, to know his comfort and his faithfulness. It never seems to fail that God allows me to feel this deep pain for awhile, but because of his care and love, he eventually lifts the stifling pain and brings me back to more of a state of normalcy.

As I have aged, I actually feel like more of a basket-case than I did when I was less mature in Christ. Funny, huh? I'm laughing as I write this now, when I think of times in the past when I have felt so out of control emotionally that I just wanted to yell and scream. I guess it's just humorous to remember how "crazy" I have felt at times. I can't even imagine how I will be when menopause hits—scary! Oh well, one thing I do know—even if I have to be admitted to the funny farm, God will still love me and keep me close by his side. Praise the Lord!

The bottom line is this: God wants us to know him and cling to him. If pain will bring us to that end, he will bring on the pain! He loves us too much to leave us pain-free.

Do you want to really know him and his faithfulness? Pain will be a part of this process. But there is hope in the great healer!

I Have Experienced the Closeness of His Comfort

Who wants to stay in their pain for very long? Nobody. Who can wipe away our tears? Jesus. Jesus is the only one who can prevent us from giving in to other things which might deliver us from the searing pain. He can keep us from sinful solutions. He can comfort us so that we don't turn to drugs, illicit sex, alcohol, food, TV, shopping, and every other type of sinful addiction. Jesus can be our righteous addiction—our holy comforter.

I do not discount the struggle that many men and women face to lay down addiction. It is easier said than done to give it up and turn to Jesus. The hurt and pain you are trying to mask through these "solutions" needs to be uncovered and I urge you to seek a Biblical counselor or minister to help you to tackle your addiction in the Lord's strength. You may be one of the Christian women in our churches that is secretly addicted to illicit sex or drugs or something so overwhelming that you do not feel you can tell anyone. I urge you to find help fast.

How does Jesus comfort us? By his Word and through his Spirit. The last thing I want to do when I'm hurting is to read the Word. What is the first thing I need to do when I'm hurting? Read the Word. We grow spiritually as we move toward his Word during our painful times instead of giving in to our pain and depression. By going to God, we enable him to comfort us.

Speaking of depression, I want to take a moment to talk about this emotion that affects so many women. Why does depression play any part in our lives as believers? Aren't we supposed to be always happy in the Lord? Depression starts with disappointment. Disappointment is not necessarily sin and is actually a normal part of life. But when we allow the disappointment to turn into discontentment and even despair, sin is born. When we don't get that "thing" that we desperately want, an idol is formed in our heart. We then become angry, dissatisfied and depressed.[4] Trust me, I know, I have been depressed many times in my life.

Let me give you an example. Several years ago, I was fortunate enough to audition for the game show *Wheel of Fortune*. I passed the audition and was called to be a contestant on the show. My quest for stardom had finally ended! I dreamed of what I would do with the thousands of dollars I might win. I did pray for opportunities to share Christ with the other contestants. But, alas, I thought more often of cash, cars and trips.

Unfortunately, I did not win the thousands but instead I

went bankrupt at a crucial moment in the game, when I nearly had $5,000 dollars in my greedy little hands. By the end of the show I had made a moderate $2,600, enough to pay for my expenses with a little left over after taxes.

For a couple of days, I wallowed in my disappointment over making a critical mistake that cost me the thousands. I had nightmares about the one word I could not figure out in the puzzle. I discovered, however, that I could either keep dwelling on the lost loot and sink further into depression or I could thank God for the once in a lifetime opportunity. After several days of sulking, I chose to honor God and give my disappointment to him. The result was a peaceful and thankful heart. (Although, it did take me a couple of years before I could watch *Wheel of Fortune* again without recalling my stupid mistake!)

Comfort comes when we give our idol over to the Lord. A demanding attitude only brings anger and dissatisfaction. "If you don't give me a husband now, God, I'm gonna… !" God can't comfort us if we hold to this attitude.

Ladies, we need to mature in Christ and trust him and his Word. Scripture puts life in perspective. It reminds us of where our hope should be. I am often drawn to Colossians 3:2 during my times of despair. "Set your minds on things above, not on earthly things." This brings comfort as I remember where my hope lies. It gives me perspective. (We will discuss more about our eternal hope in Ch. 4.)

Jesus may also comfort us in real, practical ways. He may bring a friend along who simply and sacrificially offers a listening ear. He may provide a service opportunity to get our minds on the needs of someone else. I find this one of the best comforts God uses - focusing on others!

One day, I was super sad over a guy (okay, really, I do get down about other things besides my love life!) and yet I forced myself to go to work. I was sitting at my desk at church, when I sensed the Lord pushing me to go and visit a church attendee in a nursing home. Because I was so down in the dumps, I tried to convince God this was not a good time for me to go. However, I finally obeyed the Lord's prompting and I drove over in my car. On the way, I sensed a need to sing the song "The Joy of the Lord is My Strength." Purely out of obedience, I began "singing" the normally happy-sounding tune. Because of my severe sadness, however, the tune sounded more like a funeral dirge than an upbeat melody.

I arrived at the nursing home and spent a short period of time there. The woman was very ill, so I kept the visit to a short time of Bible reading and prayer.

On my way home, as I processed this time with the hurting woman, the Lord began to lift me up. He reminded me of all that I had to be thankful for. And so I began to sing the above song again. This time, to my amazement, I made a joyful noise! I sang with all my heart and soul. God had released me from the despairing feelings in the course of hours. This was not my doing, but his. His love and power lifted me from the depths. I was half-hearted in my obedience, but he honored that itty, bitty step of faith.

God is never lacking for ways to encourage us and comfort us. One of the most harmful things we can do is to refuse to be comforted. One of the worst things we can do is to hold onto our pain and become angry and unsatisfied. Refusing to surrender our will to the Lord will only result in an ineffective and unproductive life.

Maybe you have never really felt the comfort of the Lord. The following verse is a good reminder to us that God does comfort. Second Corinthians 1:3–4 describes our heavenly Father like this: "… the Father of compassion and the God of all comfort, who comforts us in all our troubles…" The truth is that God comforts us in ALL of our troubles. Of course, we have to allow God to comfort us and not take on quick fixes instead to ease our pain.

In what ways does God comfort us? We now know that as we are obedient to reach out and serve others, even in our pain, that God's power can pull us from the emotional pit.

What are other ways that God comforts us?

The first way that God comforts us is through his directing and disciplining hand:

The 23rd psalm is familiar to many of us. Have you ever pondered on verse four of that melodic psalm? It says, "Your rod and staff they comfort me." What is the purpose of the rod and staff? For the shepherd, the rod and the staff are used to guide the sheep, driving them perfectly toward the point of destination. When we, as believers, realize that the Lord's ways are perfect and when we wholeheartedly give in to this direction, there is comfort and joy. We do not need to figure out for ourselves which way to go. We can trust the God of the universe who sees and knows all to pick out the perfect job or ministry for us. We can call on him to pick out the best mate for us when and if that time comes. We can even ask him for help to pick out a doctor or dentist. And you thought 1–800-dentist was revolutionary!

Growing up, I would have never considered a career in inner-city youth work. I wanted to be a dancer or an actress. At sixteen years old, I first laid my eyes on Michael Jackson's *Thriller* video. It was then that I discovered my calling. I would be a music video backup dancer. One year of jazz dance lessons at Gretchen's School of Dance and I was ready! As I matured in Christ, however, God implanted in me a passion to do God's will, no matter where that would lead. God was faithful as I sought him through prayer and godly counsel to direct me toward full-time ministry. He placed things across my path to direct me toward his will. I read *The Cross and the Switchblade* by David Wilkerson and my eyes were opened to the needs of the inner-city.

As a junior in college, I changed my major from Business to Sociology because of God's prompting. Sociology further opened my heart to the plight of the poor. Several years later, I traveled from California to Chicago to begin the career which *God* chose for me. He is so good to put us where he wants us if only, like sheep, we will follow faithfully to the place where he leads. Take comfort that because God knows you better than you know yourself, he will graciously guide you to the perfect destination. Isaiah 30:21 says, "… you will throw them away like a menstrual cloth and say to them, 'Away, with you!'" (Oops, that was Isaiah 30:22.) This is what verse 21 says: "Whether you turn to the right or to the left, your ears will hear a voice behind you saying, 'This is the way; walk in it.'"

Even when God uses that rod and staff to discipline us, we are comforted. I know that when God's Spirit speaks to me about my sin and won't stop talking until I listen, that God loves me. I am comforted to know that God will not shrink back from disciplining me when I need it. His love will not allow that.

The second way that God comforts us is through the reviving power of his Word:

Psalm 119:50 says, "This is my comfort in my affliction, that your Word has revived me" (NAS). How does God's Word revive us? What does the writer of Psalm 119 say? "I delight in your decrees" (vs. 16). "My soul is consumed with longing for your laws" (vs. 20). "I will meditate on your decrees" (vs. 48). "I have sought out your precepts" (vs. 94). We are comforted and revived by God's Word as we meditate on it and fully allow it to penetrate down to the deepest part of our hearts. Try it! There is no comfort to the troubled soul like the piercing Word of God! Oh, Lord, pierce our hearts with your Word. Comfort us to the depths!

Another time when I was feeling supremely wounded after breaking up with a special someone, God wooed me to his Word. I remember crying and screaming and even hitting the 1970's wood-paneled walls in the flat I was renting at the time. I was totally tired of letting go and letting God. Instead I was in a fighting mood. I was mad at God. I didn't trust his judgment. God let me throw a fit that day. He waited while I wailed. He listened while I yelled. He let me live even though I verbally pummeled his character. After some time, I thought of getting my Bible. I said to God, "I'll go get the Bible, but it ain't gonna help!" I opened the Bible and began reading a passage like Isaiah 40:11 "He tends his flock like a shepherd: He gathers the lambs in his arms and carries them close to his heart." At first I refused to be comforted. I said something like this to the Lord: "God, you're mean. You do not care for me like you do one of those cute little sheep!" But as I read and reread several piercing passages of scripture, God melted my heart like a pat of butter in the summer sun. He reminded me of his love and my heart fluttered with joy and trust in the midst of sorrow. Draw nigh to the Words of God!

The third way that God comforts us is through people:

II Corinthians 7:6–7 reads, "But God, who comforts the downcast, comforted us by the coming of Titus, and not only by his coming but also by the comfort you had given him. He told us about your longing for me, your deep sorrow, your ardent concern for me, so that my joy was greater than ever." God comforts us when someone else cares. I have a plaque in my house given to me by my grandmother. It reads "What a world of woe lifts from our hearts when we really know that somebody really and truly cares, that we're in somebody's thoughts and prayers (Author unknown)."

I am normally the type that prefers to cry alone. I feel a comfort level with the Lord that I don't always feel with others. I would rather only him see me when my eyes are swollen and snot is bubbling out of my nose. But during one time of woe, I called my friend Kim at 1:00 a.m. to "cry on her shoulder." She quickly wakened her heart and mind and listened to my tragic tale. She offered words of comfort but mostly listened and cried with me in my late-night hour of need. It's a beautiful blessing when someone is truly concerned for your well-being, feels your pain and desires to bring you comfort. Thank God for the times he has sent someone in your darkest hour to encourage, comfort and strengthen you.

Of course, God's comfort is not only for the purpose of making you feel better. II Corinthians 1:4 continues, "so that we can comfort those in any trouble with the comfort we ourselves have received from God."

I Have Comforted Others with the Comfort I Have Received From the Lord

Just the other day, I was speaking with a first-time attendee to our church. She was in the midst of several trials that were completely overwhelming her. She felt frozen—utterly unable to make decisions or even do daily tasks. In addition, she felt consumed by a deep feeling of loneliness. She lived with family and was often in the midst of people but felt so lonely that it was driving her to desperation. Could I feel for her/relate to her?

I won't pretend that my problems were as difficult as hers were—drug addiction and an impending move to name a couple—but I can say that I have felt deep loneliness. On that level

I could feel her pain and know how she struggled to not give in to hopelessness.

Fortunately, I also know a God who has delivered me and sustained me in deep times of loneliness. This gave me the ability to comfort her and encourage her because of the way Christ had comforted me and encouraged me in the past. I didn't just offer her advice on an intellectual level. I was able to feel for her and offer hope because of how Jesus had given me hope.

Imagine how Jesus must have felt when he considered his impending torture as he battled in prayer at the Garden of Gethsemane. Imagine the loneliness that he felt when his disciples couldn't even stay awake to pray for him. Imagine his loneliness when he realized that no one on earth knew what he was going through and would go through. Imagine his loneliness when he knew that shortly he would be separated from the only one who could understand his pain—his own Father. Can Jesus comfort you in your time of loneliness? I think he has the "credentials" to be able to do that. If you have been through loneliness or some other deep struggle, don't you think that God wants to use you to comfort someone else? Dear single sister, allow Christ to develop the credentials in you that you might be used mightily by him to comfort another in her time of desperate need.

I Have Grown in Trust of Him and Full Dependence on Him

"Trust in the Lord with all of your heart and lean not on your own understanding. In all of your ways acknowledge him and he will direct your paths." Proverbs 3:5–6

I wish I was perfect at trusting in him and relying on his plan. I caught myself even today just rolling over and over in my mind issues of guys and singleness. I am often trying to figure things out for myself instead of leaving things at his feet and walking away.

But I am growing, I think, to depend on him and trust in him. Remember that Philippians 2:13 says, "For God is at work in you to will and to act according to his good purpose." Even though today I feel less trusting than I did three days ago, I can see a more trusting spirit developing over the long haul. I am thankful to the Lord for this. Do you trust God more than you did when you were first saved?

I am thankful that in my single state at age 39, I can trust that he has not made a mistake in my life. I am thankful that he is working out everything in my life to accomplish his good purposes. I am thankful that I don't need to figure out what the future holds (although I try) but that God has my life mapped out. I am thankful that what God has orchestrated in my life is GOOD.

It doesn't always feel good. Even today, I am feeling some-what sad in the place that I find myself—a little lonely and won-dering when and who God will bring to fill this empty space in my heart and in my home. But I know that I don't have to get stuck in these feelings. I can depend on God to raise me up, encourage me and give me a higher purpose which will move me out of my sadness.

I thank God that we have someone who is dependable, trustworthy and good. Lord, please help us to get beyond ourselves and look to you for life—the life abundant that you promised!

I am Growing in Finding My Hope in Him and Him Alone

The key words here would be, "I am growing." I wish I could say that he is my all. I wish I could say that he is my all sufficient fullness. I wish I could say that I have found him to be my only hope. I cannot say these things. But I can say that he is showing me as life goes on that he is the only one who can truly fill, who can truly bring joy. In Proverbs 13:12 we read, "Hope deferred makes the heart sick." I've felt this. My hope to be married has definitely been deferred! But should this be my ultimate hope? I don't know that it is wrong to desire and to even hope to be married. But this should not be where my ultimate hope lies or else I may be stuck with a sick heart for the rest of my days. I don't want that. Do you?

I think our hope needs to be based on something else, something bigger. Romans 5:3–5 says,

> Not only so, but we also rejoice in our sufferings, because we know that suffering produces perseverance; perseverance, character; and character, hope. And hope does not disappoint us, because God has poured out his love into our hearts by the Holy Spirit, whom he has given us.

Hope is based on God's love for us that has literally been poured into our hearts. We need to learn to drink from this deep well of God's love instead of trying to find our hope in so many other things. The next time singleness sadness hits you between the eyeballs, stop, put down your purse and cancel your trip to the mall. Don't give in to the temporary solace of the shopping center. Instead of shopping 'til you drop, sit with God in the silence. Wait for his comforting Words to penetrate and heal your hurting heart. Josh Groban's song *You Raise Me Up*[5] expresses perfectly God's ability to lift us out of the mire. "When I am down and, oh my soul, so weary; When troubles come and my heart burdened be; Then, I am still and wait here in the silence, Until you come and sit awhile with me. You raise me up, so I can stand on mountains; You raise me up, to walk on stormy seas; I am strong, when I am on your shoulders; You raise me up: To more than I can be."

We need to bask in his Word to get to know this love, this hope that does not disappoint. Take a moment now to consider what your hope is in. If it is not in Christ, ask God to work in you that your hope may be in the only one who has the power to give you hope!

God has called me to be single for now. How do I know this? Because I am single! Today I live as a single Christian woman loved and cared for by the God of the universe. He has a purpose for this calling. Are you called by God to be single for today? Ask him to strengthen you to accept this call wholeheartedly for today. He is able!

The Temptations

Temptation #1–Adultery/Sexual Immorality

Edith Wharton writes a tale of longing and destitution in her book, *Ethan Frome*.[6] My heart cries out similarly to that of the title character, Ethan. Although Ethan is not single, he is married to a cranky, sickly woman. Each day is lived in unhappiness and discontent as he resides with a woman who lives only to please herself. His world is brightened, though, when his wife's niece, Mattie, comes to live with them. Ethan longs to talk to this girl, even hold her and kiss her, but it is a forbidden love. As the book is read, the reader cannot help but feel for Ethan, stuck in a loveless marriage with the girl of his dreams so close by, yet so unattainable. I weep even now as I think of the longing in my heart to know the love of a man and how I have considered compromising God's call to experience this. In the not-so-distant past, there was a man—a temptation to some degree such as Mattie was to Ethan. I share the following personal struggle only to show the deceitfulness and longings in all of our hearts that, if not shielded, can lead to destruction.

Jack is a man I had interacted with at a place where I love to exercise. For a long time it had been an innocent hobby, one that had fulfilled my passion for sports and given me an arena to share the gospel with the unbelieving. But then temptation crossed my path in the form of an unsaved, married man. (Now, keep reading and try not to be too shocked at my openness. Although temptation may or may not have visited you in this same way, if you are growing in the Lord, the enemy will pull out all of the punches to try and take you down!) I didn't begin speaking with him thinking, "Oh, I think I'll fall for an unsaved, married man." But over time, the longing grew as the sinful thoughts unsuspectingly popped into my mind. My desire to interact with this man grew as the desires in my sinful heart began to take over.

In *Ethan Frome*, Ethan, gives into these sinful longings, thinking continuously of Mattie, fantasizing of a future with her and finally, in the end, giving into the temptation by kissing her and expressing his feelings to her.

STOP! What does I Corinthians 6:18 say? "Flee sexual immorality." What does Paul command Timothy to do in II Timothy 2:22? "Flee the evil desires of youth." (Okay, I know I'm 39, but I can't seem to get over that "desires of youth" thing.)

As much as my sinful nature would have loved to "pull an Ethan Frome," I am thankful to the Lord that the voice of the Spirit is louder than the lust of the flesh. Praise God! When the idea of simple obedience just isn't enough to lure our sinful hearts into submission, we must pull out all of the stops. To continue even speaking to this man could have eventually ended in a kiss, an affair or, just as bad, an affair of the heart. *It could have ruined a family, wrecked a ministry, stifled the Spirit, derailed God's plan, and taken advantage of the grace of God.* To this point Jack and I had only just conversed. For all I knew, he had thought nothing of our interactions, but it was my heart and thoughts that were at stake.

So God spoke, and slowly but surely I heard and obeyed. First, I had to go to the facility at certain times to avoid Jack. Next, as the avoiding got harder to do, I felt the Lord gently but firmly asking me to step away from this beloved activity for a time. And so I did. I stepped away from this place of temptation for several months and practiced resisting the devil. God asked of me a difficult thing. He asked me to give up something I loved and to even give up opportunities to share Christ with others that I might not fall. My flesh would have rather given in to the Harlequin Romance fantasy and stayed put. But God instilled in me a stronger desire to obey. The battle of the wills raged but, as mentioned above, God's voice and Spirit proved louder than the lust of the flesh. "To him who is able to keep you from falling" (see Jude :24a) is a promise I cling to. HE IS ABLE, HE IS ABLE! And when we yield to his will, even giving over those things we "love," he gives peace, joy, and satisfaction. As we walk in his perfect will and serve him in complete surrender, we can avoid the devastation of sin. He is able to give victory out of the sinful longings. When we experience God's power to rescue us from our sinful selves, we can also encourage others in their battles with the flesh. We can encourage other single and married women toward purity and righteousness. In the heat of their battle, we can proclaim, "God will help you fight your battle with the flesh. Fight, woman, fight! Don't give in to Satan and his schemes to take you down!"

God gave me peace when I obeyed him and fled temptation. What a relief to not feel the constant battle of sin waging war in my heart. As I look back on that temptation, I can almost say that I am thankful that it took place. First of all, I am humbled because of my own vulnerability. I will never look at another person's struggle and think—"I would never be tempted by that!" And second, I now know that God can pull me out of a very scary and potentially sinful place. He is so good! Is God calling you to get away from something or someone so as not to fall into sin? The peace that the Lord brings as you are obedient far outweighs the temporary pleasure of sin. His ways are always better than our ways. I beg you to listen to God and to obey quickly. Your heart will heal as you let go of that someone or something. God will place his joy in that empty place in your heart.

There is no greater peace than being in his will even if his will is to be single, even if his will is to struggle with this "thing" for all of this short life, because the important thing is his glory. Our hearts speak to us differently, but we know the truth. We have his perspective. His Word is enough. To God be the Glory.

Let us also consider other temptations that ebb and flow through the life of a single woman.

Temptation #2–To marry a man who is less than God's best

I admire Sarah and Abraham for waiting on God as long as they did for the child that was promised to them. Unfortunately, they didn't wait quite long enough. And because they took things into their own hands, there were bitter consequences. Sarah grew tired of waiting for God to provide her with a child and so she came up with a plan to give her husband children through Hagar, her maid. The result was not the blessings and happiness she had hoped for, but misery, jealousy, relational problems, anger and other sinful actions and emotions (see Genesis 16).

Samson also ran headlong into sin and temptation. God had commanded the Israelite people not to intermarry with women from other nations. (See Exodus 34:15–16 and in I Kings 11:1–2). However, Samson refused to consider any of the "saved" women of his time, the Israelite women and chosen ones. He went against God's command and connected himself with a Philistine woman named Delilah. Unfortunately, Samson's disobedience resulted in his own death (see Judges 16). He, too, took things into his own hands and suffered deathly consequences for it.

There is a temptation out there for the single woman to distrust God in the area of her love life. There are many saved and growing, believing women who sacrifice all to be with someone who is not God's best. Why do many women make this devastating mistake?

Disappointment with men in the church

I am realizing that sometimes we single women have unrealistic expectations of men in the church. (We do need to have high expectations of men, just not unrealistic.) Now, I understand that there are just some good-for-nothing men in our churches (just like there are some good-for-nothing women). There are some wolves in sheep's clothing that use the church to take advantage of unsuspecting sheep—and some of these sheep are the weak-willed women that are mentioned in II Timothy 3:6. Certainly we need to use caution when interacting with such men.

However, many of our brothers are growing in the Lord just like we are and are making mistakes along the way. I think we women need to realize that sometimes we hold onto unrealistic expectations of where men should be spiritually. Maybe you compare your single brother with your pastor who seems so consistently on fire for the Lord. Maybe you compare him with that caring deacon who is always visiting the shut-ins. We need to be careful not to compare our brothers with others but to look more often for how the Lord is changing them to be more like Jesus.

I think we also expect men to communicate the same way as women do about their relationships with the Lord. So when a man gets more excited about discussing a particular doctrinal issue than discussing how the Lord has been their strength in times of trouble, we are disappointed, sometimes wrongly, believing that "those guys just don't care about the Lord as much as I do!" Ladies, it may appear that maturing Christian single women outnumber maturing Christian single men, but I beg you not to play the numbers or to be discouraged by statistics. If it will bring God glory to marry you off, he will bring it about—no matter what the odds! (Disclaimer: If you never leave your house or step foot in a church or comb your hair or take a shower or talk to men—you get my meaning—even God is going to have a difficult time hooking you up; he doesn't always choose to perform miracles!)

Even though I am 39 and unmarried, I still believe that in all things God's timing is perfect. I may marry at 42 or 45 or 50 (I may have to hit some more walls if I have to wait until 50!). Others may think, "She's getting married a little late, but isn't it cool how God finally brought her a man!" God says, "My daughter, I am never late or behind. Here is a blessing at the perfect time." As believers in Jesus, we can always trust, always hope, and never give way to fear because God is working such amazing purposes in our lives. Okay, I feel like I'm going to cry. The thought of God's goodness mixed with the Luciano Pavarotti CD I'm playing is driving me to tears. (That Pavarotti, he is so sneaky!)

Desire for sexual intimacy

People at my church probably look at me and think—"She is so godly. She probably has no sex drive. She probably doesn't struggle with that and is so content in her singleness. What a godly, pure, no-sex-drive woman." I'm kind of exaggerating, of course, but for those people who don't really know us, it is easy for them to form ideas of what our struggles may or may not be. I think we all do this to some degree.

Well, thankfully, I will spare you the details of my sex drive. But the bottom line is this—God created all of us with a drive for sex. God can seem unfair in calling us to wait to fulfill this desire. Although I don't fully understand why God would give us this desire and then not fulfill it, I do know that this unful-filled desire has potential to develop in us one particular fruit of the Spirit.

This really hit me a couple of years ago when I woke up at 5:30 in the morning to the loud sounds of my neighbors having sex. I was thinking to myself, "I am trying to stay away from TV, music and movies that promote lustful thinking. But now, I have to literally get up and leave my own room!" Yes, I was a little angry that I had to endure this kind of "alarm clock."

I just love, though, how God can take everything, if we allow him, and use it for good. I realized at that moment that I was still responsible to have self-control. If this happens again, I need to be quicker to get up and get away from the offend-ing noises. I still need to take my thoughts captive and make them obedient to Christ. One of the things I did do during those moments (while plugging my ears) was pray for those so near to me. I knew they were not married, so with a kind of righteous anger I began praying that they might be convicted of the way they were living their lives. I know this sounds kind of funny, but I am so thankful that God can use any situation as an opportunity to pray!

Galatians 5:22–24 says,

> But the fruit of the Spirit is love, joy, peace, patience, kindness, goodness, faithfulness, gentleness and *self-control* (emphasis mine)… Those who belong to Christ Jesus have crucified the sinful nature with its passions and desires.

I am not saying that sex is sinful, but it is sinful outside of the context of marriage. And it is sinful to compromise and marry someone just because of our own selfish desires, whether they be sexual desires or otherwise. Paul does say in I Corinthians 7:9, "for it is better to marry than to burn with passion." However, this does not give us the freedom to marry anyone we want without consulting the Lord. God knows our sexual struggles and will bring someone along if the struggle is too much to bear.

I encourage you to work on the fruit of self-control if you are struggling to remain sexually pure. For the woman who craves attention from men and uses her sexual prowess to get that attention, I challenge you to ask God to purify your heart and motives. I encourage you to practice loving others more than you love yourself. Whatever your sexual struggle, I encourage you to plead with the Lord to help you to manage this area of your life.

Attention from ungodly men that you are
not getting from godly men

Our single brothers in Christ have a hard job. They are called to be above reproach when it comes to single women. At the same time, they are challenged to communicate care and concern to their single sisters in the Lord. I don't necessarily envy their responsibility. I think sometimes we, the single sisters, can become discouraged from the lack of attention we are receiving from the opposite sex in the church. In a perfect world, our brothers would be perfectly loving and caring without coming across as "too interested." But let's face it; our brothers are walking in different levels of maturity and different personalities. Many are still learning how to interact with us ladies as sisters in Christ. We need to give them grace because it is not an easy calling. How often do you pray for the single brothers in your church? Ouch! We need to do this more often.

Do you seek attention from a man at work because you are not getting it from the men at church? Do you hope someone will notice you at the health club since no man in the singles group is looking your way? Do you say yes to a friend to go to a club because of a deep longing for a man to take initiative with you? The single woman who is craving male attention may decide to take things into her own hands and look for a man of the world because she is just not willing to wait on God to provide her with a God-fearing gentleman.

What is this deep longing in our hearts? Sometimes I just ask myself—why do I want some attention from a man right now? What is this deep need in my heart that so desperately longs to be met? Why did I get myself extra "prettied up" today so that I would be noticed?

I offer some reasons why we may crave male attention

1. The need to feel needed: Genesis 2:18 says, "It is not good for the man to be alone. I will make a helper suitable for him." God planned for woman to help man. And, boy, does he need it! (Just kidding!) Is it possible that women were created with an innate need to help a man? I am just offer-

ing this possibility—one reason why we have this longing in our hearts to connect with a man. Remember, though, we are not all the same. We desire to help in different ways. We have various gifts and abilities. Some of you love to serve. The idea of serving your future husband—bringing him his bathrobe, slippers and remote control, thrills you to the very core of your being. Others of you have the gift of giving. You get excited about getting your future husband the perfect birthday present—perhaps a little homemade love coupon good for ten free backrubs. And then there are women like me who have the gift of teaching. I look forward to teaching my husband a thing or two! Ha, Ha! But seriously, women help in all sorts of different ways. As single women, we are empowered to help many people using the precious gifts God has given us.

2. The curse: Genesis 3:16 says, "Your desire will be for your husband and he will rule over you." I understand that for centuries Bible scholars have been trying to figure out this verse. Is it possible that the desire we have for an intimate relationship with a man originated in the very beginning— even back to the curse? As I sit here in Starbucks, staring out at rush hour traffic on a beautiful November evening, I am happy, but there is a part of my heart even now that is craving the company of a man. I was just recently telling a friend that every fall/winter I yearn to get dressed up and go on a date. I don't know why the yearning suddenly hits me in November—it may be the idea of a nice restaurant with a cozy fireplace—ooh, la, la… romantic! Anyway, is it a curse or a blessing to walk around with this craving? In some ways, I am thankful for it because it draws me to Jesus—it is yet another opportunity to commune with him and allow him to fill me. Okay, honestly, I'm really not

this emotional, but I feel some tears welling up once again when I think about the sweet times I have had with Jesus as a result of this longing. Wow, if Peter, Paul and Mary had not just come on over the loud speakers singing *Puff the Magic Dragon*, I might have had a full-blown emotional attack right here in Starbucks. Where is Pavarotti when you need him?!

3.   The society: We are so self-focused. We are constantly considering our own happiness. Therefore, since movies, billboards and music pretty much tell us that a man will bring that happiness—there you go! We have to fight against this societal message. In addition, our society subtly whispers this lie. If men desire to be with us—if we're peppy, pretty and popular enough—we are worth something. Certain women do have a certain magnetic affect with guys. I admit, I am sometimes jealous of that kind of charisma and/or beauty. But then I remember that God created me with purpose from and passion for Jesus. I wouldn't trade that for all the beauty in the world!

4.   The desire for the Lord: II Corinthians 5:4 says, "For while we are in this tent, we groan and are burdened, because we do not wish to be unclothed but to be clothed with our heavenly dwelling, so that what is mortal may be swallowed up by life." Maybe some of these unfulfilled longings and groanings for a man are actually a deep desire to be with the Lord. "Lord, fill us with your presence even now."

Let's meditate on the following verses in the Psalms right now. They remind us that God can meet the deepest needs of the soul. Psalm 63:3,5: "Because your love is better than life, my lips will glorify you… My soul will be satisfied as with the richest of foods." Since David was a king, it may have been difficult for him to have a real friendship with a woman, or even a man for that matter. True, he had an amazing friendship with Jonathan, Saul's son, before becoming king. But it appears his royal position probably brought less opportunities to get together with homeboys and homegirls for coffee. Hence (I just had to use this word once in the book), he was forced to look to God for his comfort, guidance and soul satisfaction. What an exceptional example of one who found the Lord sufficient even in the deepest parts of his soul.

Satan desires to "sift you like wheat" by using temptation #2—settling for less than God's best. Keep that in mind the next time you are craving a man's attention and are tempted to give in to any Billy, Bob, or Burt that happens by!

Temptation #3—To take matters into your own hands

A newly married friend of mine looks back on a particular mistake she made while still single. Before Eliza met her husband, she wasted emotional and spiritual energy obsessing over another man who was not God's best for her. But she had to have him. She did not say that out loud, but her actions and emotions told the real story. She had fixed her eyes and her hope on this individual and did what she could to obtain his affection. They were friends, but she wanted more. She subtly manipulated her way into this man's life and heart. The things she did would not hold a candle to the manipulation tactics that the world has to offer, but she knew then and knows now that the initiative she took to attempt to secure this man was sin.

The following statements demonstrate the subtle pursuing and manipulating that Eliza now regrets and that many of us single women are tempted to engage in.

1. Location Manipulation: "I would 'accidentally' end up sitting next to him in church." "I would 'coincidentally' run into him after an event or worship service."
2. Flirtation Manipulation: "I would pass him and initiate a light brush on the shoulder."
3. Passive Pursuit: "I would ignore him, but then look around desperately to see if he was watching me." "I told him that I had feelings for him and couldn't be just friends. I did this in part to determine whether or not he had feelings for me."

For Eliza, the above behaviors demonstrated lack of trust in God and dependence on self. I admit I have also participated in some of the above subtle manipulations in order to make something happen. Sometimes these subtly aggressive behaviors may even work in drawing in the man. This is what occurred with Eliza. The man she so desperately wanted did become her boyfriend for a season, but the relationship ended in much pain and regret. Eliza partially attributes the unnecessary pain and hurt, both in and after the relationship, to her own sin. She desperately wishes now that she had not taken matters into her own hands.

Ladies, we need to analyze our motives and repent from selfish scheming. Do you believe that God can bring you together with another man without your help? Can he burden the heart of your future husband to take initiative with you? Please stop now in any subtle pursuing you are doing and repent before the Lord for the times you have taken things into your own hands. Please hear me, single sisters. I am *not* saying you should never talk to men or look for opportunities to meet them. I *am* saying that you need to allow God and the man to be the initiator of the romantic relationship. Now, take a deep breath and tell God that you trust him to bring someone across your path that will pursue you in his perfect timing if that is his will.

I share the following story from *Believing God for His Best*[7] by Bill Thrasher to encourage us to be honest with God about the subtle scheming we are tempted to take part in.

> For me it was during 'break' times that my need for companionship was accentuated. During a two-week spring break in March, I needed to go through my library and catalog it. I thought of a sweet Christian girl who might be very helpful in this project. In fact, it seemed like a great idea! Later, I was meditating on Matthew 4:1–11 and noted that Satan's first temptation was directed in the area of Jesus' obvious need. I felt that if I had fasted forty days and nights and someone suggested to me to turn stones into bread (and if I had the power to do so), I would genuinely thank them for the suggestion. Christ's response was different. Christ recognized that He was being tempted to take matters into His own hands. He was being tempted to act independently of the Father. In the same way, on the surface there was nothing wrong with asking the Christian girl to aid me. However, God showed me that it was a 'self-effort scheme' to meet my need for companionship.

Repeat after me: I will no longer, by the grace of God, manipulate or pursue a man to get what I want. I will trust God. I will wait on God. I will not take matters into my own hands. I will include God in every step I take and each decision I make regarding the men who capture my attention.

Temptation #4—To lead a life of self-absorption

People are like sponges. I know you have probably never

pictured yourself as a sponge. Perhaps you have envisioned yourself as a picturesque paper towel, but definitely not a holy (I mean holey) sponge.

A sponge can come in all shapes, sizes and colors, but one thing all of our sponges have in common is their ability, or shall I say talent, to soak up stuff. All sponges were born to absorb. (I hate to even think of the sponges that were born to absorb and yet are never used for this purpose, perhaps being wrongly used as makeshift earplugs or, even worse, lying dormant in a store with no purpose—but that's another book.) Some of our smaller sponges are really only outfitted to soak up small amounts of liquid, while some of our larger, more hefty sponges are quite useful to soak up the worst of messy spills.

Like sponges, people are born to absorb and then wring out. Although we also come in many shapes and sizes and colors, our sole purpose is to take in Christ and then to "wring him out."

What happens when we are not absorbing Jesus and instead are absorbing self? Well, I know you are no dummy, but let me tell you—YOU are wrung out! So, guess what? Other people get to see more of you and less of Jesus. What a lovely thought. Can you just picture all of your nasty habits and sinful emotions being laid out for the entire world to see? Not a pretty picture, is it? Let me explain a little further.

Singleness shouldn't mean I get to do whatever I want whenever I want. As believers, we should have a different view of our freedom from marriage and family.

It is unfortunate, but some singles are more of a detriment than a benefit to the kingdom of God. Are you one of those singles who is using all of your free time for selfish pleasure and entertainment, being so absorbed with your own fun and happiness? Think about what you did this past week. How much time did you spend: With the Lord? Going out to eat with friends? At the movies? Watching TV? Serving with your church family? If you spent more of your time doing entertainment-oriented activities, then you desperately need to consider reordering your priorities.

James 3:16 says, "For where you have envy and selfish ambition, there you find disorder and every evil practice." Do you battle to serve the Lord wholeheartedly rather than serving self? I know I do. I guess most do—some more than others. I consider myself to be a very selfish person and, trust me, I am not bragging. This is one of the many characteristics about myself that I am not too thrilled about and that God has continued to work on.

So as I write this section, I admit, I am a work in progress in this area. I'll even admit that I have used this weakness in my life to try and convince God that it would be better for me to be married. "God, I am convinced it would be much better for me to be married because then I would finally be dragged out of my self-absorption!" So far, God has not bought this reasoning. He's probably laughing (with me, not at me) at the various arguments that I have come up with, including this one, to try and convince him that I should be married.

Have you noticed that when you give in to selfish desires, you often come away empty? For me the bottom line is that the more I mature in the Lord, the more it hurts when I am disobedient. I am realizing more and more that God desires to be master over all of my time—not just 50% of it or whatever amount I choose to give to him that day. We are on this earth for such a short period of time relative to the time we will spend in heaven. We have only so much time to serve Christ and to accomplish things that will benefit his kingdom. Think on this for a moment. We will give an account for the time we spend here on earth. Again, single and free person, recall what you did with this past week. How much of your time was spent for the benefit of God's everlasting kingdom? Were you absorbing Jesus and then wringing him out?

I know one thing I struggle with is watching too much TV. I'm not going to lie, I like watching TV—I really enjoy it. I am a sucker for reality shows that involve some kind of competition. My favorite is *Amazing Race*. But I am also easily sucked into *Survivor*, *Fear Factor* and even *The Apprentice*. Because there are a lot of these shows out there, it is a battle to keep the TV off. God has convicted me on this many times. He is probably getting tired of telling me to turn off the TV. Now, I'm not saying I watch hours and hours a night, but even one to two hours a night is time that could be better spent reading, calling someone or studying the Bible. Of course, I realize that some of you don't struggle with this at all. I come across some people who convict the socks off of me when they say, "Oh, I used to watch TV, but it's not a temptation for me anymore." I feel like such a schmuck when I consider that I have not been better at laying this habit aside. But, God is working on me, and as I realize the time he gives to me is sacred, I spend it more wisely.

Maybe your entertainment isn't TV. Maybe it's going out to movies, hanging out with friends (because you're more social), or playing games on the computer. I think many of us have things that we do in order to escape or enjoy life. I'm not saying this is always wrong, but anything in excess poses a danger of making our lives less fruitful.

Dear sponge of God - I challenge you to fight against self-absorption. I challenge you to absorb Jesus. Dwell on him. Think on his attributes. Practice living as Jesus lived. As you wring out Jesus into the lives of those around you, many will taste his living water. They will be reborn, renewed and re-energized into abundant life with Jesus.

The temptations that I have discussed above are real. The enemy will try and use them as you battle to live fruitfully as a single. Thankfully, God is much more powerful than the enemy and he can and will bring victory out of the temptation if we surrender to him.

The Benefits

I know that many of you do not care to acknowledge that there are any benefits to being single. You just want to be married! However, many of you who are reading this ARE single. We don't know about tomorrow or two months or two years from now, but today you are single. Don't you desire to live life fully rather than whine away your precious single days, months or years? Okay, pray for a right attitude and let's go...

I wonder whether married people are afforded as much opportunity to daydream as single people. My friend Julie, who was single until her early 30's but is now married, says, "My mind sometimes wanders back to the days when I was single. Back then, I often basked in thoughtful moments of reflection. That definitely isn't happening now with a husband and kids! I am forced to wake up before everyone else in the home just to get a few solo minutes with God. I long for more alone time to ponder and pray."

There is nothing like those precious moments at home, blasting upbeat tunes while reflecting on my day. The music creates a communion with God that words cannot express. (The spell is only broken when suddenly the CD changes to Toby Mac and I am compelled to dance around the house like a Solid Gold dancer!) I am one satisfied single when swaying to the peaceful piano in one of Fernando Ortega's "road trip" songs. I call them road trip songs because when I am listening to them, I suddenly want to jump into my car and drive somewhere…really anywhere. Unfortunately, I am not spontaneous enough to actually ever do this! I am currently listening to one of those songs entitled *California Town*. I am from California, so the lyrics draw out fond memories of driving up and down that beautiful state, listening to music and talking to God while on my way to visit family and friends.

I love these moments alone with God to daydream and meditate on him. It is no-cost therapy to spend time thanking him for what he is doing in my life. As *difficult as single living can sometimes be, I am grateful for moments of solitude and times of reflection that may not be as available to those who are married with kids.*

There are definitely benefits as we walk through this life as single people. God even tells us in his Word that there are advantages to living single.

It is Better to be Single

How many times have you been sitting in a church service and you realize the sermon topic for the day is something like "Singleness, the Better Way to Go"? Not very many times? When I think back on my thirty plus years in church, I can hardly remember even one sermon encouraging the single to remain single and reminding the congregation of the benefits of singleness over marriage.

On the other hand, how many times have you been in a church service and the sermon subject addressed marriage in some way, shape or form? If you're like me, you might be able to think of even a couple of times in the last year when marriage was the topic of the morning message. Let us look at what Paul has to say about singleness in I Corinthians 7.

Many of us have heard that it is better to marry than to burn with passion. I Corinthians 7:9 says, "But if they cannot control themselves, they should marry, for it is better to marry than to burn with passion." So we know from this truth that—in today's manner of speaking—it is better to get married than to live forever with an out-of-control sex drive.

But what else does Paul say in his letter to the Corinthians? "Now to the unmarried and the widow I say, it is good for them to stay unmarried as I am" (I Corinthians 7:8). Paul says it is good for the unmarried to stay single. It is good. What does good mean? Not bad? Actually, more than just not bad. Not bad would be more neutral. The dictionary definition for good is: 1. morally excellent 2. proper or fit. What are some other things that were called good in the Bible? Let's see: creation, God, Jesus, the gospel and the list goes on. I think this puts singleness in pretty good company!

Singleness does have benefits. Over the course of this chapter, we are going to think positively about our single situation. What are the advantages of living the single life?

Benefit #1–You can have undivided devotion to the Lord

I Corinthians 7:34–35, 38: "An unmarried woman or virgin is concerned about the Lord's affairs: Her aim is to be devoted to the Lord in both body and spirit. But a married woman is concerned about the affairs of this world - how she can please her husband. I am saying this for your own good, not to restrict you, but that you may live in a right way in undivided devotion to the Lord. So then, he who marries the virgin does right, but he who does not marry her does even better."

. . . Before I elaborate on these verses, I cannot help but

stop for a moment of silence and offer my condolences to the waiting virgin that looked forward to marriage with this godly man. I can picture the scene. This innocent woman is grinding grain one day when her man comes running in to her after a long day out in the fields. She looks up at him with a hopeful smile on her face realizing that, in a couple of months, the home they are building will be ready and they will be husband and wife, living in bliss under one roof. But to her dismay, the first sentence out of his mouth is "I have decided to remain single and serve the Lord." She drops her grain grinder and falls to the floor distraught. Her hopes of life as a married woman are now but a thing of the past. This moment of silence has been brought to you by Grain Grinders Inc. where grinding grain is our greatest aim...

Okay, wipe those tears now. Let us return to our passage.

What is Paul's motive for saying these things? One motive is "that we may live in a right way in undivided devotion to the Lord" (I Corinthians 7:35).

The following are two ways devotion to the Lord may be achieved in the life of the single woman.

1. Serve Unreservedly

Although there is loneliness associated with being single that sometimes drives me to consider marrying the next guy I see walking down the street—ha, ha! (probably an advantage of not being so spontaneous)—there are benefits and good feelings associated with being the master of my life, so to speak. There are just more choices. For instance, I can choose at the last minute to participate in outreach at my church on a Friday night. Paul did say it is better to be single than to be married and even though I hate to admit it, I see why.

Let's face it, we have more time to serve more people.

And there is joy in that. To be used in a variety of different ways by the Lord is exciting. Now, I am not a natural "server." God had to drag me screaming to begin to serve people. And it still doesn't come naturally. I am not a "yes" girl. I always have to think before I tell people I will do something. But I am so thankful to God that he has been so persistent in my life to put service opportunities in my path so that I would learn that we are made to serve. I have come to the conclusion that a person who doesn't reach out and serve others will never really live a full life. Even just today, as I was having more of a self-centered day—shopping, reading, etc., I have come to the end of my day feeling like something was missing. I'm pretty sure that the empty place in my heart is a result of doing many things for me but not much for others. So if you are single, serve. If you're dying to get married and feel so down because there is no one around, ask the Lord for a ministry. Don't allow your emotions to dictate your actions. Reach out. Watch for opportunities.

The following scenario demonstrates how God can use you to reach out to others.

> The church is having a day of evangelism which will include a class on witnessing and then a time to go to the local park and share Christ with people.
>
> *Married woman*: (to her husband) "Honey, you can go to the evangelism day. I'll stay home and watch the kids."
>
> *Single woman*: "I am a little nervous but excited to step out in faith as we share Christ! I'll be there!"

It is not uncommon for me to be able to participate in a service opportunity at church while my married friends need to stay home with their husband or kids.

You may be saying, "But I don't want to go to the evangelism day!" "I hate talking to people I don't know." "I wish I had kids to stay home with and take care of." I challenge you to renew your mind with godly thoughts. I challenge you to look at service opportunities as opportunities to grow. I challenge you to work on walking as Jesus walked. He was single and yet did not grumble and complain but looked at each part of life as an opportunity to build relationship with the Father and glorify him. We need to get it out of our heads that it's some kind of curse to be the one that is available to serve. Some singles complain, "Why do they expect me to help just because I'm single?" Instead, let's be thankful that we are available to serve because, with the correct attitude, we can be truly blessed!

2. Spend Time with the Lord

The book *The Five Love Languages*[8] by Gary Chapman helps us to understand that each person experiences love in different ways. I think that one of my love languages is quality time spent. In other words, I feel that if someone truly loves me they will make the effort to spend one-on-one time with me. I'm guessing that many women would claim this to be one of their love languages. I went to dinner and a movie with a friend the other night. Because I don't go out to see movies very often, much less dinner and a movie, I was so excited! I thoroughly enjoyed the personal conversation with my friend over Chili's fajitas and bottomless cokes. No, we didn't talk that much about men! And then to top it off, we enjoyed a clean, entertaining movie that we could appreciate together and talk about afterwards. I thank the Lord for the quality time that we had. I am especially excited when I get together with my female friends and we make a point to pray together at the end of our time. I try to do this most of the time when I get together with friends. It really gives the time eternal value when we can bring the things we have talked about to the throne of grace. As single people, not only can we have more undivided time with friends, but we can also choose to take advantage of our days and have consistent, undivided time with the Lord. The Lord promises from Jeremiah 29:13 that "You will seek me and find me when you seek me with all your heart."

Let's remind ourselves why we should even be drawn to spend time with the Lord. Jeremiah tells us that in seeking God, we find him. In spending time with the Lord, we come to know our Father and Savior. The following excerpt from *Come Away My Beloved*[9] by Frances J. Roberts speaks from God's perspective in good, old-fashioned English.

> Thou dost not need to carry thine own load, for I will be happy to help thee carry it and to also bear thee up as well. Thou dost not walk alone nor meet any situation alone, for I am with thee, and I will give thee wisdom and I will give thee strength, and My blessing shall be upon thee. *Only keep thine heart set upon Me and thine affections on things above; for I cannot bless thee unless ye ask Me and I cannot answer if ye do not call, and I cannot minister to thee except thou come to Me.*

I love being able to settle down and ask God to speak to me and to help me to sense his presence. I can then dig into his Word and wait to hear his voice. I was speaking to a woman in church this past week. She was asking for prayer that she might have a more consistent time with the Lord. She was trying to get up in the morning to spend time with Jesus, but her husband would often want to talk with her and interrupt her during that time. She was feeling a little frustrated with this distraction. During my times with God, I do have to deal with my own restless heart desiring to get up and get on with the day, but I don't have the tension of a husband or child interrupting. I don't have to take a phone call that someone else answers because I can choose to not answer the phone. I won't experience an intrusion from my husband who is reminding me—nicely, of course—that I forgot to make his lunch. I am not being rushed with my time in God's Word because my five-year-old is knocking wildly at my bedroom door while screaming that his pet hamster fell into the toilet. I am completely and totally the Lord's for that period of time. *Ladies, we are not lacking in relationship because we are not married. We have an opportunity to cultivate the most fulfilling relationship possible – with Jesus, our God and our friend!*

Check out the following responses to another true-to-life scenario:

> Two women are tired from the long day. They have a lot on their minds. They both desperately desire to pour out their hearts before the Lord and spend time in solitude, meditating on his Word.
>
> *Married Woman*: "Let's see, I still have to cook dinner, get the kids' baths and stories before bed, get lunches ready for tomorrow…Lord, I need your touch, comfort and encouragement. When will I find time to meet with you?
>
> *Single woman*: "What a day—my heart is so heavy. I can't wait to get home, kick off these shoes and grab my Bible. The phone calls and laundry can wait until tomorrow. Lord, thank you that I am free to meet with you now, when I so desperately need you!"

I have not shared these scenarios to discount the tireless work of the wife and mother, but to remind you, the single woman, that you do have more opportunities to be devoted to the Lord. Remember, it is not just me saying this. First Corinthians 8:35b says, "… that we may remain in undivided devotion to the Lord." God longs for us to be undistractedly devoted to him. Pure devotion to God produces life, love, joy, peace, wholeness, contentment, and soul satisfaction. Now this is definitely good!

Benefit #2—You can know God as your Husband

When I was less mature in the Lord, I used to hear women say, "God is my husband" and I would think to myself, "What are they talking about? They are just lying to themselves so they won't fully experience the hurt of not having a husband! They are just trying to 'buck up' and sound spiritual. Yes, God is your provider, your comfort, your guide, the one who loves you more than anyone else, but your husband? Please!" However, as I have matured and have spent time reflecting on what I desire in a husband, many, if not most, of those qualities are found in God! In Isaiah 54:5 it is written, "For your Maker is your husband— the Lord Almighty is his name."

God has so faithfully provided for my needs as a single person that it is as if I had a perfect husband taking care of me 24/7. And I'm complaining because I'm single? Well, there's still the physical intimacy stuff, and I haven't quite figured out what God is going to do about that, but I'm sure he'll help me to deal with that struggle for as long as I remain in this single state. Anyway, back to the husband thing. Here are a few ways God has proved to be the most faithful husband a woman could ask for!

I have been a missionary in the inner city of Chicago for about eleven years. I have never in that entire time gone without a paycheck. I have never been without food, clothing, shelter, and other needs and plenty of wants. The Lord has even provided me with enough money to buy a place of my own. Before owning this condo, I had super cheap rent in a lovely two-flat building. God has also provided me with a car that was sold to me for way under the blue book value and is totally reliable.

I thank the Lord for each one of his provisions. I Timothy 6:17b says, "… who richly provides us with everything for our enjoyment." Now, don't get me wrong, I'm not promoting a health and wealth gospel here. If all of my earthly goods were stripped away, God would continue to provide for my needs in creative and unique ways. Maybe you have a testimony as to how he has done that. The key here is that God honors our faithfulness—the little bit of effort we put out to trust in him and to be obedient. Don't miss that part. If as a single person you are still trying to run your own life and you come up wanting, it is not due to a lack of heavenly provision. It may be due to your lack of effort to trust God with your life and/or your refusal to let go of sin. "Lord, we thank you for giving us some of those cattle on a thousand hills and that you take care of us so richly, even though we are so undeserving. You are a good God. Thank you for caring about even the hairs on our heads."

My Companion

Have you ever been home on a Friday night and wished you could be somewhere else, preferably on a date with a gorgeous, godly man? (Actually gorgeous is not important—just godly and not completely unattractive.) I know this has happened to me more times than I wish to admit.

I remember one such time that I was feeling lonely. I was on the internet checking my email and one of those advertisements for eHarmony.com popped up. So I clicked on the sight. They had one of those deals where you could actually sign up for the basics for free. So, I went forward and filled out the whole questionnaire, doing so without consulting God. Suddenly, I was available for all of those eHarmony men to read about. Over the next couple of days, I had fun reading various bios and wondering if I really could move to Hawaii if that guy was "the one." However, after praying and considering whether I should contact any of the prospective men, I sensed the Lord was not freeing me up to do so at this time. So I quietly withdrew my information without ever having contact with anyone. For me, my short stint in the internet dating world came about out of a time of loneliness. It was not the best way for me to respond to my loneliness. I was not trusting God at that moment but trying to take things into my own hands.

I am not saying that joining a dating service or chatting on the internet is always wrong; however, if you are doing it out of loneliness, without consulting God, it is an opportunity for the enemy to get a foothold. This is not a book on dating, but I caution you, woman of God, to be very careful if you decide to meet men online. Our world is such that even the guy who appears quite trustworthy and "normal" online may be exactly the opposite in person. On the other hand, I know that there are men and women who have met one another in this way and are glorifying God in their marriages today. So, may God direct each one of us as we seek him for a marriage partner.

Most of us would rather run away from an impending wave of loneliness than allow it to crash mercilessly on top of us. Most people will do anything to keep from experiencing loneliness, especially if they have previously experienced its powerful pull into pain. It is not a good feeling. It is not a happy feeling. It is a crippling emotion that doesn't go away easily. And yet I am thankful for having experienced this feeling. God has shown me his faithfulness in times of deep loneliness. He has lifted me up and given me hope. He has even filled my heart with joy out of these times.

As spoken of briefly in the previous chapter, it is simple how the Lord accomplishes this. As loneliness seeps into my inner being, desperation is born. I wander aimlessly around the house seeking something, anything to fill the empty space in my soul. Like an addict foraging for her next fix, I am in dire straits thinking of who I can call or where I can go to get rid of the awful feeling. As the loneliness continues to set in, thoughts of God mix with futile contemplation. I think of his faithfulness in the past. I consider opening his Word. He burdens my heart to run to him. This is the way God woos me. His still, small voice becomes too persistent to resist, so I approach my Bible and open it. I begin to read his Word and meditate on it. The truth begins to sink into my soul and soon I am reminded of God's love and his great concern. Verses like these allow me to speak freely to the Lord of sadness and longings:

> Psalm 30:2: "O Lord my God, I called to you for help and you healed me. O Lord, you brought me up from the grave; you spared me from going down into the pit."
>
> Hebrews 4:16: "Let us then approach the throne of grace with confidence so that we may receive mercy and find grace to help us in our time of need."
>
> Psalm 34:15: "The eyes of the Lord are on the righteous and his ears are attentive to their cry."

I am not trying to present to you a formula for how to feel better in times of loneliness and depression, but God will meet you in the dark times—give him a chance.

Go to his Word. Read a few verses. Meditate on them. Ask God to quiet your heart. He will show you that he can be the best and greatest of companions you have ever known. Honestly, there have been a few times when I have been experiencing the joy of the Lord as I spend time with him and I think to myself, "I am better off than my married friend '*so and so*' who is probably watching a boring movie with her husband right now!" Or, more realistically, she is probably running after the kids, while trying to wash the dishes, while doing the laundry, while cleaning the house… you get the picture! Thank you Lord that you are able to be my friend and my companion!

My Caretaker

Lastly, I am thankful to God for taking care of my daily needs. Like a helpful husband, the Lord has made sure I have received help with day-to-day necessities.

About a month ago, my bathtub was seriously clogged. Since I no longer live with my handy ex-roommate, Amy, I was in dire need of an unclogger. And since I own this condo, it was really up to me and not a landlord to deal with this. The amazing thing is that the developer of the condo was more than happy to send his son over with a bathtub snake to fix the clog. They have no obligation to help me since the condo unit is my responsibility, but not only did the son bring the bathtub snake over to fix the tub, the dude totally got dirty and fixed the clog himself. I didn't get one bit of black bathtub backwash on me! I am so thankful to God for providing men who are willing to help out in my time of need. God does take care of his children. He has also provided me with an earthly father who I can call on at any time with questions about my house or my car. I am thankful for parents who are concerned even about the most trivial needs in my life. *God really is like the perfect husband in so many ways. He never complains when I ask for help. He never says he's too busy to take care of a need. His provisions never run dry.*

His love for me never grows cold. He never threatens to disown or divorce me. He is the perfect lover of my soul!

Benefit #3—You can have less trouble in life

A second motivation Paul has for encouraging us to stay single is that he desires to keep us out of trouble! Paul tells us in I Corinthians 7:28, "But if you do marry, you have not sinned; and if a virgin marries, she has not sinned. But those who marry will face many troubles in this life, and I want to spare you this." Paul is thinking of our good when he encourages the unmarried to remain single. He desires to spare us from trouble. What might some of these troubles be in the 21st century?

The trouble (or struggle) of:

1. Remaining purely devoted to one person for life
2. Learning how to relate to and live in harmony with a person of the opposite sex
3. Learning to submit to your husband and to the Lord at the same time
4. Dealing with the consequences of your spouse's bad decisions
5. Shielding your godly, or not-so-godly, husband from not-so-godly women
6. Agreeing with one another on various decisions that need to be made
7. Watching your husband struggle to be the spiritual leader of the home
8. Trying to agree on what raising godly children actually looks like
9. Agreeing on how to handle the finances

And number ten: drum roll please…

10. Continuing to have to put the toilet seat down!

And the list goes on from here. You get the idea. Living closely with another person brings additional problems in life. Of course, it's not wrong to be married, but with marriage comes added difficulty in life. Again, God inspired Paul to write this.

In the Church

There are many well-meaning, mature Christians in our churches who will neglect to tell you these things. They will tell you that marriage is good (which it is) and will tell you they are looking out for a husband for you or praying and fasting for a husband for you. But what they often forget to do is encourage you in your singleness and remind you that it is good—well, *according to God's Word, actually better than being married.* They forget Paul's teaching and often assume that it is best for you to be married. Well, let's be honest. Wouldn't you rather hear someone tell you, "It's okay, sweetie, God has a wonderful husband out there for you somewhere!" as opposed to, "Oh, deary, you know it's better to be single, so enjoy it to the fullest. I'm not going to ask God for a husband for you because that would not be the best." We want to hear that marriage is going to come our way—that God is waiting for the perfect time to send that perfect someone. Why do we want to hear these things? Because what Paul is proposing—to purposely remain single—is a hard teaching. Not many are ready to lay down their lives to this extent.

Most of us don't really love God quite that much, myself included. "Thank you, Lord, that although some will not understand and some will even look down on us because we are unmarried, as singles we can live in undivided devotion to you!" I'll admit that even as a 39-year-old-should-be-content-by-now single, I don't want to hear that remaining unmarried is good because I want to somehow convince God that it is better for me to be married. I definitely hope that God will at some point look at me and say, "That girl is just burning way too much with passion—I better quick send a godly man her way!" But until that time, I am thankful that God has counted me worthy to be wholly devoted to him.

"Lord, we thank you for the many ways that you take care of us single women. Help us to be thankful for your loving care and not complain because of what we do not have."

Take some time now to make a list of the benefits that are part of your single life. And then thank God for those things.

I'll get you started:

- More time to cultivate a relationship with Christ
- More time for hobbies and interests
- More ice cream in the freezer!

Keep going. You can do it!

The Eternal
Mindset

Set Your Minds On Things Above

Do you know this song? "When I get to heaven, gonna walk with Jesus. When I get to heaven, gonna see his face. When I get to heaven, gonna talk with Jesus. Saved by his wonderful grace. Because I'm saved, saved, wonderfully saved, washed in the blood of the lamb, hallelujah...."

It is important that we view our singleness in light of eternity. Colossians 3:1 gives us this command. "Since, then, you have been raised with Christ, set your hearts on things above, where Christ is seated at the right hand of God." It is when I become self-focused and this-world-focused that I am especially vulnerable to feeling down and discouraged because of my singleness. Therefore it is imperative for me (and you) to keep this verse close at all times to maintain a godly focus.

Here are some additional verses that encourage us to focus our eyes on things above:

1. Matthew 6:20: "But store up for yourselves treasures in heaven, where moth and rust do not destroy, and where thieves do not break in and steal. For where your treasure is, there your heart will be also."

Wow, convicting. If my heart *demands* to be filled by a man, I am obviously trying to obtain the wrong type of treasures.

2. Matthew 6:33: "But seek first his kingdom and his righteousness, and all these things will be given to you as well."

In Matthew 6, Jesus promises us that he will provide for our daily necessities. I know what you're thinking, "Yippee, he is going to provide the money for my satellite TV!" I am not happy to be the one to inform you of this, but here it goes—satellite TV, Moose Tracks ice cream, Express jeans, and Starbucks coffee are not included on God's official list of necessities. But the point remains, and it is a simple one to grasp. All we have to do is seek after God and his kingdom. God will provide whatever else he thinks we need. So don't worry, be happy in the knowledge that God is taking care of you, every moment of every day if you simply trust and obey.

3. Mark 13:31: "Heaven and earth will pass away, but my words will never pass away."

What is going to last? God's Word will never expire. It is probably a good idea, then, if we dwell on it and ask God to help us to believe it with all of our hearts.

4. John 6:35: Then Jesus declared, "I am the bread of life. He who comes to me will never go hungry, and he who believes in me will never be thirsty."

Let us remember that God is able to be all sufficient for us while we walk this earth.

5. John 6:38: "For I have come down from heaven
    not to do my will but to do the will of him who
    sent me."

Are you self-serving in your desire for a mate or do you
desire to do God's will whatever that may bring you? What is
your reason for wanting to be with someone?

Let's talk about #5 a little longer. After all, whether we
desire to be married or desire to remain single—it should be for
the right reasons, for God's eternal purposes.

Nate, a friend from church, once challenged me with the
following questions: Why do you want to be married? Do you
understand God's purpose for marriage? Do you understand
what your role in marriage will be?

These questions triggered deep thoughts in my simple
mind. Prior to the encounter with Nate, I had not been dwelling on how I could glorify God if I was married. Frankly, I
was fixated on how MY needs would be better met if I had a
man around. This brother was not sharing with me something I
had not considered previously. But the questions resonated at a
deeper level in my brain this time. I didn't simply reply, "Right,
uh, huh, I so get that!" But I went home that evening and satu-
rated my thoughts and prayers in the Ephesians 5 verses on
marriage.

The book of Ephesians written by Paul gives us such a
great picture of what marriage is all about. After I received
the above challenge from my brother in Christ, I went back to
Ephesians 5:22–33 to wholeheartedly dwell on God's purposes
for marriage. (Side note: Did you ever think how great it was
that Paul, a single dude, was giving "advice" on marriage? You
go, Paul—and Nancy Leigh Demoss!)

The whole purpose of marriage is to demonstrate Christ's relationship to the church. This is so cool, I can barely stand it! I think this makes a great case for asking God to bring you a marriage partner who will be able to love you as Jesus loves. This also means that you need to be actively practicing submissive behavior so that your future marriage will be a picture of the church submitting to Christ.

Lately, I have been trying to make a conscious effort to be submissive to authority in my life. I work at a church and, as is the case in many churches, there are a significant number of men in leadership positions who also work there. This gives me plenty of men in authority with which to practice submission. So far, I have probably failed to be submissive more times than I have succeeded. I think there is a part of me that wants to prove that women can have an opinion, too, and so I allow little things that I am asked to do to get me riled up instead of just being gracious and obedient. I may often come across as one with a quiet and gentle spirit, but when another brother or sister in Christ comes across as prideful or dogmatic concerning a certain issue, I suddenly possess a less quiet demeanor and a more loud opinion! There is nothing wrong with having an opinion and sharing that opinion—it is all about how we do it, ladies. Am I speaking out of defensiveness or out of love? Am I trying to squelch someone else's pride or am I trying to encourage them? Is there someone in your life with whom you can practice submission?

Even though I have failed at the submission test more than once, I am excited to practice this and to become better at submitting myself to others. After all, the Bible says in Ephesians 5:21, "Submit to one another out of reverence for Christ." This means we should be in the practice of submitting to one another in the body of Christ at large. So we really have plenty of opportunities to practice. If you are not connected with a local body of believers, here is yet another reason to do so. If you cannot submit to authority or other believers in the church, how do you ever expect to be able to submit to a husband?

Okay, back to number five. Who dictates your life? Is it you and your selfish desires? Or do you desire to do the will of God? If there is even a part of you that desires God's will in your life, he will be faithful to make your desires his desires. I know, because I have seen God do this in my own life. And I know he doesn't love me more than he loves you—so if you ask him, if you plead with him to give you a desire to do his will, he will answer your cry and give you his desires.

You can start by asking God to help you to understand his will more deeply in regards to marriage. Isn't it exciting to think that if God chooses to bring a husband into your life that you can totally glorify him through that marriage? As long as we remain single, it just gives us more time to prepare for marriage. Watch out all of you excellent husbands to be!

Set Your Minds On Others

When I have an eternal focus, my focus will automatically shift from me, me, me to you, you, you. "Each of you should look not only to your own interests, but also to the interests of others" (Philippians 2:4).

I have been so affected lately by the stories I hear of other people's suffering. In addition, when those stories are of people who are unsaved—without Jesus—it just breaks my heart. I was watching Oprah the other night and the topic of the show was child molestation. It sickens me how many young girls have been molested in our country. I'll be honest, I sometimes wonder why God allows this evil to happen. But we know that God can use even *this* evil for good in the lives of those who trust in

Jesus. As I watched Oprah, the opposite appeared to be true. One of the women who had been molested seemed lost in this pain, even after confronting her abuser. There wasn't a sense of hope or closure. There wasn't a sense that she expected healing from the horrific tragedy. That bothered me. I desire for others to know Jesus the way I know him, so that no matter what horrific life experience they encounter, they may still feel joy, peace and hope.

When I see or hear about the sufferings of others, it puts life in perspective. When I hear about a Chinese Christian that has been jailed for the umpteenth time because he shared his faith, my focus moves heavenward. When I hear about children in other countries who have lost both parents to AIDS and are trying to survive the disease themselves without their mom to hold and comfort them, my prayers shift outward. When I walk down the streets of Chicago and pass a drug-addicted woman who can barely walk straight, my motivation for ministry moves forward.

My "need" for a husband suddenly becomes less important when I am privy to the more desperate needs of others. *When I stop and consider that so many people need to know Jesus, I am more motivated to pray for the lost and less motivated to pray for the man of my dreams. I am more motivated to spend time sharing Christ with my neighbors than to spend time looking for a husband.*

Where is your perspective? Are you only seeing life through your own lenses? Do you need to put on Jesus glasses that you might view life through his eyes? "Lord, we ask that you will give us eyes to see as Jesus sees, with an eternal perspective. Give us hearts that hurt not only because of our own pain but because of the pain of others. Give us minds to dwell not only on our own needs and wants but on the needs and wants of others. Give us compassion not only for our lost family members or friends, but for our neighbors, our co-workers, and strangers that cross our paths every day. Give us not only eyes to see you working around us, but courage to join you in the fight for souls."

Set Your Minds On Jesus

Hebrews 12:2 says, "Let us fix our eyes on Jesus, the author and perfecter of our faith…"

Do you remember that Jesus was single? True, he died at 33 years old. But he lived a single life in a day and age when most men and women were married in their teens. The way that Jesus lived his life as a single, godly man for 33 years is definitely something we need to check out. Let's take some time to learn from the greatest single man of all time!

First of all, in case you're not convinced that Jesus has something to teach you in the singleness department, let me ask you these few simple questions:

- Do you ever complain about being single?
Jesus never did.
- Are you ever mad at God for calling you to live as a single?
Jesus never was.
- Do you ever battle with sinful depression and anxiety as you wait on God's best?
Jesus never did.
- Are you ever bored with life because you don't have a significant other to share it with?
Jesus never was.

Oh, and please do not say that Jesus can't relate to you. "He was tempted in every way, just as we are—yet was without sin." Hebrews 4:15b (Just a friendly reminder)

If you answered yes to any of the above, you definitely need singleness advice from Jesus. Let us see what he has to say:

Dear Jesus,
I'm a 42-year-old single woman who is lonely and longing for a husband. I am tired of living life alone and yet wonder if there is a way I can be happy and content as I am. What should I do? Signed, Looking for Love.

Dear Looking for Love: "If you remain in me and my words remain in you, ask whatever you wish and it will be given you" (John 15:7). Practice living the scriptures and God will give you joy and contentment if you ask him. So now, I hear the question coming: "Is it okay to ask for a husband and will he give me that also?" This is the deal. Only God knows if you and marriage will mix well. So, soak yourself in his Word and then ask the Father if it's okay for you to pray for a husband. In time, he will burden your heart one way or the other. He will prompt you to pray according to his will.
Love, Jesus

Dear Jesus,
I'm a 30-year-old single mother of two. I am so tired of raising these kids on my own. But it seems impossible that any man in his right mind would choose to marry me with all the "responsibilities" I have. What should I do? Yours Truly, Fed Up and Frustrated.

Dear Fed Up and Frustrated: I know how you feel. I didn't have a human partner to help me teach and train my disciples. Every day I was with them, trying to help them to walk righteously in the sinful world. But my Father was always available to me and I called on him often. Now that I am interceding for you at the right hand of the Father, you need to call on me anytime you're in need. "Come to me, all you who are weary and burdened, and I will give you rest" (Matthew 11:28).

As for the second part of your question, I say, "…with God all things are possible" (Matthew 19:26b). If it is the Father's will, he is more than able to accomplish it.

Love, Jesus

Dear Jesus,
I am a divorced woman in her 30's. I love to go out on the town and have a good time. But there are no men in my church who are asking me out. I am tired of just hanging out with the women and playing board games. What should I do? Sincerely, Alone and Bored.

Dear Alone and Bored: "Go and make disciples of all nations, baptizing them in the name of the Father and of the Son and of the Holy Spirit, and teaching them to obey everything I have commanded you." It sounds like you are very much a people person and enjoy leading a social life. That's good. I am all about people, too. I would challenge you to switch your focus from how your needs can be met to how you can meet the needs of others. Go out on the town! Learn how to talk to people about the Lord. Take an evangelism class at church. Look for someone who knows less than you about the Lord and start meeting with her to help her walk more like me. The Father desires to use your social personality to reach out to others in my name. Go to it!

Love, Jesus

Correct focus is so crucial when it comes to any type of success. As I write this, the 2006 Winter Olympic Games are going on in Turin, Italy. I am constantly amazed by the athlete's ability to pull off a winning performance in the face of nerve-racking competition. The downhill skier careens down an icy mountain at 70 miles per hour with precise muscle control and concentration. The figure skater lands perfectly on the ice after rotating three times in the air with thousands of eyes fixed on her every move. The short track speed skater pumps his burning legs around treacherous curves at 40 miles per hour while others skate precariously within inches behind and in front of him.

Our success as single adults also depends on our focus. Are you dwelling on things above? Are you looking out for the needs of others? Are you fixing your eyes on Jesus? If so, you will experience success. It is true you may stumble and even fall at times, but over the long haul you will glorify God and live a life worthy of his calling. Keep your eyes on the prize—focus on eternity!

The Thoughts

While growing up in central California, summer temperatures often lifted above 100 degrees for several days in a row. Because of the pull on energy sources during this season, our family participated in an optional program that curtailed the energy output during times of high usage. This program would save us money, but force our air conditioner to shut off during hot times of the day.

Wouldn't it be nice if our brains could sign up for a similar program? It could be called the "stop your thoughts to conserve brain juice" program. During certain times when thinking spirals out of control, our brains would simply shut down to save the in-demand brain juice. No longer would we play victim to the smattering of thoughts that walk nonchalantly into our brains without being invited.

Have you read any of the Harry Potter books by J.K. Rowling? In her book *Harry Potter and the Goblet of Fire*[10] Professor Dumbledore uses his wand to extract certain thoughts from his brain and stores them in what is called a Pensieve for later use. Professor Dumbledore explains to Harry Potter, "One simply siphons the excess thoughts from one's mind, pours them into a basin, and examines them at one's leisure."[11] It certainly seems like it would be helpful on occasion to store thoughts to consider at a later date. But, alas, we have not been given wands or Penseives to accomplish that feat.

Thoughts can breed so many different emotions and physical abnormalities. Trust me, I know. I am the queen of obsessive thinking, especially when a guy enters the picture. We know now that the curse may have something to do with why we struggle so much for male attention, but is there another reason? I think so. Let's look at that reason.

The Boy Box

For centuries scientists have done studies on the human brain. Many facts about the brain have been uncovered that help us understand how we think and why sometimes we don't think. One such study has determined that most individuals only use a very small portion of their brains. If you look at the human race today, I believe that discovery has been confirmed!

Unfortunately, there is one part of the human brain that not only hasn't been a part of scientific study, but, sadly, most scientists don't even know exists. Perhaps this is because a large percentage of neurological scientists are males. Therefore, they have not even considered this sensitive area of the brain. It's a pity and a shame, but I am writing to divulge something to you, the reader, about this little known area of the brain I call the Boy Box and what is scientifically referred to as Quadralateralis Homosepias.

Who of the human race has a Boy Box included in their brains? The large majority of those who are privileged to possess this delicate area of the mind are females—mainly single females between the ages of 12 and death.

What is the Boy Box? What is its function? I'm glad you asked. This is an area of the single woman's brain where male prospects are thought of and considered. It is the area where one or more particular males may reside in any individual single woman. It is an area of the brain that will control many other areas of the body if not kept under control by the larger part of the brain.

Here's how it works. You get up one Sunday and go to church. You are introduced, quite innocently, to a particular single man in the singles group who is new and appears quite nice and charming. You think nothing of him until you meet a second time and have a 20 or 30 minute conversation. Again, you go about your usual Sunday routine and wake up early for work on Monday. At work on Monday, you are busily working and all of a sudden, HE pops into your mind—no, not Jesus of Nazareth, but the guy you've talked to twice and have learned that he is saved and likes to read short novels and watch long movies. That is pretty much all you know. Of course, you ask yourself, "Why am I thinking about this guy—I hardly know him?"

Little do you know, he has secretly and unsuspectingly slipped unnoticed into your Boy Box. It's a regretful thing because he begins to take up part of your thinking space. I can testify to this because I have someone in my Boy Box even now. Yes, this is someone I have only talked with a few times at church and hardly know anything about, but my Boy Box and all the mechanisms included with it have helped to turn this acquaintance into even a potential marriage partner. The Boy Box is tricky and will create something out of nothing; therefore, it is extremely important to keep this Boy Box and all of its contents, whether it be the thoughts of one, two or many individuals, under control.

Another captive of the Boy Box might be a man whom you have actually befriended over time. In this case, sometimes the Boy Box may resound with thoughts such as, "I wonder if he would be interested in me in a romantic way?" "He sometimes takes time to talk with me at church—maybe he likes me." "He did compliment me on my outfit once—maybe that was a hint that he is attracted to me." This friend-turned-love-interest can also be a source of contention for the brain. This boy in your Boy Box also needs to be kicked right on out of there until he actually makes a declaration with words of his intentions to pursue you romantically.

Second Corinthians 10:5b says, "… taking every thought captive to the obedience of Christ." Ladies, do you take that command seriously? I am battling with this command even as I write this. I desire for my thoughts to be pleasing to the Lord. I desire to be pure in my thinking about my brothers in Christ, whether single or married. I desire to not jump ahead in my brain with thoughts of marrying someone especially before I even know him. I trust that God knows my desire to please him and that he is helping me to get control over these displeasing ways of thinking. I cringe to think of how many men have been in my Boy Box at one time or another. I am ashamed to think of how I have thought of some men who later became the husbands of other women. I thank God for his forgiveness and patience with me in this area. *TIP:* While my friend, Eileen, was single, she would struggle with attractions toward various men as many of us do. She would often remind herself that those men were quite possibly future husbands of other women. This helped her to keep sinful thoughts to a minimum and regard those men as brothers in Christ.

Are you one of these women who is consumed with thinking about a particular man in your life? Sister, don't give up. God wants you to have victory in this area. How does this victory come? How do you purify/clean out your Boy Box? It's a simple method, really, albeit difficult to apply. Here are the step-by-step instructions:

Boy Box Purification Procedure

Step One–Consider the reality of the situation

Do you know this man? Can you justify thinking about him 24/7? Do you know beyond a shadow of a doubt that this is the man you are going to marry? Do you know that God is leading you toward this man?

If you answered no to any of the above questions, you need to douse your Boy Box with a dose of reality. We need to tell ourselves the truth. In my case, I need to remind myself of things like: I don't know him. I have no right to be thinking of him in the ways I have—as a future dating partner or husband. I do not know if he is the best one for me. God desires for my thoughts to be of him, not of some stranger that I may or may not come to know any better in the future. In your case, you may need to repeat to yourself things like this—this guy has not declared any intention to pursue me. I need to not read into every move he makes toward me. I cannot figure out this man's intentions. I need to dwell upon Jesus, and, if necessary, even spend less time with a man that may be knowingly or unknowingly toying with my emotions.

Step Two–Oust unproductive thinking out of the Boy Box

During a short season of my seventh grade year in school, I managed to acquire some enemies. A little gang of three "stoners" began stalking me. (The term stoner was used in the 1980's to describe people who hung out after school, smoking cigarettes, stealing bikes, getting into fights and the like.) The gang consisted of a skinny blond girl, an oversized brunette girl and a long-haired boy who was probably six inches shorter than me. I have no idea why they began picking on me. Perhaps I was an easy target. At any rate, anytime I found myself in their presence, there was name-calling and intimidating. Shockingly, they even wrote such words as scuz and scum on my locker. This little war came to a climax when, after school one day, I got into a confrontation with the boy "stoner." Fortunately, I avoided an all-out fight by hitting him several times with my enormous 1980's-sized purse and running away. Following this demonstration of my purse-wielding capabilities, these three evildoers went on to torment some other nerdy kid.

We need to be this aggressive with many of the detrimental thoughts in our Boy Boxes. We must battle them with all of our strength. I don't normally promote violence, but sly and sneaky thoughts need to be dealt with head on. Imagine clobbering those thoughts with a baseball bat or backpack filled with heavy books. A beating like that will definitely send those thoughts to the thought graveyard.

Step Three–Meditate on scripture when thoughts of this boy enter the Boy Box

After the ousting process, we need to replace our wrong thinking with the truth. The Boy Box is only so big; therefore, when God's Word comes for a visit, any lingering boy thoughts are forced to leave.

Step Four–Consider the calling of God on your life

What is your purpose? I have talked with several young women over the years who were sure that they would be married and have kids in the near future and so have given up on seeking God for any other purpose in their lives. Of course, it is quite possible and even highly likely that many of these women will get married and have kids, but should this be the main goal and purpose for their lives? I answer with a resounding NO! The immediate purpose for these women should be to follow God with their whole hearts. They should seek to serve him through the local church as they go about school and work in the world. They also need to be praying desperately for God to reveal a calling for their lives. God does not desire for us to just wait around for marriage as if that's the final frontier. Yes, the plan for you may be to be married—but perhaps he has an additional purpose for your life that he desires for you to discover. Don't just stand there waiting for Prince Charming to sling you up onto his horse and take you to paradise—look now for ways God desires to use you, a unique individual, to build his kingdom. True paradise—walking perfectly in God's will and using the gifts he has generously lavished on you—is waiting at your doorstep!

Step Five–Pray for God's divine help and intervention

The Boy Box can be controlled, but only God has the power to really help you bring this part of the brain to an inactive state. We need God's help. "Lord, we pray to you even now that you would come to our aid. Please help us as we so desire for husbands. Please give us your grace as we try and dwell upon you and make you the owner and controller of our Boy Boxes. You are able. Amen!"

Consequences

What are the consequences of not keeping the Boy Box under control? Of letting it take control? Of not giving the contents over to the Lord? Some of the consequences may include anxiety, depression, anger, and jealousy. Let's talk a little about each of these.

Anxiety

I think anxiety may increase as we get older—in regards to singleness, anyway. The male prospects decrease. Our biological clocks are ticking. It can become more of a "desperate" matter to find a mate, before it's too late.

My parents, who live in California, were recently trying to sell their camping trailer. They advertised it in many places but sadly there was not even one person who was willing to make the purchase.

Finally, months later, they advertised it again at a significantly lower price and, low and behold, they enticed a buyer and the trailer was sold, much to their relief. No longer did they have to pay a storage cost on the thing or worry about how they would "get rid of" this monstrosity.

Often, for the older single woman, there are not many "prospective buyers" who come along. So, if one does come, it can become a matter of life and death to entice that interested party.

It is very difficult to wait on God. It can also be very difficult to wait on the man. I went through a situation not too long ago that required me to wait and, in hindsight, I wish I had waited better.

As you know, I am 39 years old. So last year, when a 33-year-old Christian man approached me to ask me out on a very low key group date, I was first of all taken off guard. However, as I prayed about it, I felt like it was okay to go ahead.

We went and it seemed to go fine for the most part—although a difference in doctrine came to light. I left thinking nothing would happen between us, which at that point was fine with me. To this point, I was actually keeping a level head and was able to go on with life as is.

However, two weeks later, he called again and we began to talk. Then over the course of the next week or so I began to get attached to him—too fast. But because of the doctrinal difference between us, we really couldn't move forward in our relationship. I could see my emotions veering out of control before my very eyes.

I began to get anxious. I couldn't sleep at night. My appetite was decreasing. And all because of a man that I had only recently started to get to know.

Why did I have all of this anxiety? Basically, I knew it then and I know it now. There were two reasons. One, I allowed my Boy Box to take over the majority of the other areas of my brain. I began to think of this man considerably more than what was called for in the situation. The second reason why I became full of anxiety was that as the Boy Box took over, I struggled to trust in the Lord. Instead of allowing God's Word to dwell in the forefront of my mind, I allowed fears to consume me. Would God rip this man out of my life like he had done with all of the other men? Would this man choose instead a younger, prettier girl? Would I end up deciding to date this man, or even marry him, only for him to be the "wrong" guy?

Fears like these and others overtook my mind—or should I say, I allowed them to overtake me. I did try to some degree during this process to trust the Lord and to renew my mind with his truth. I attempted to dwell upon such Bible verses as Philippians 4:6, "Be anxious for nothing, but by prayer and petition, with thanksgiving, let your requests be known to God…" and I Peter 5:7, "Cast all your anxiety on him, because he cares for you." And there was some victory in this. But the anxiety continued which then lead to....

Depression

In chapter one, I already talked about how depression works. When something we want becomes something that we must have, it becomes an idol of the heart. When we don't get that thing that we believe will make us happy, depression may set in.

As I became more and more anxious about the situation

and gave in to my fears instead of trusting in God, not only did I become exceedingly anxious, but I also became depressed. My hope was in this man. My hope was in marriage. My hope was not in Jesus. Although I desperately wanted my hope to be in Jesus, the desire for marriage became bigger at this time than my desire for God.

Jealousy

I noticed also during that time that I was prone to jealousy. I saw him talking to other women a couple of times and I had to fight jealous thinking towards those women. I really did try to attack wrong thinking in my brain. After all, I knew that the Lord had said, "Do not be jealous. Put on love." However, it became a battle of the mind to look at certain women with love and not with a jealous eye.

All of these negative emotions were initiated by what may have seemed to be a minute mistake at the time. I did not take control over my Boy Box. I allowed myself to think of a man who I barely knew as a potential marriage partner.

God's Intervention

Fortunately, God showed me something huge during this process. He showed me that when I cannot seem to get a grip on my own, prayer and God's power can bring victory. I felt the Lord prodding me to humble myself and ask for prayer from my church staff during this time. I did not tell them any of the details of my struggle, but they were gracious enough to lay hands on me and pray for me. After this humbling of self and time of prayer, I saw God's power take over. My anxiety went away. God gave me wisdom in the situation. I was no longer depressed.

It was only days later that the gentleman and I talked and agreed that it was not going to work out to pursue anything between us. But, praise God! I had peace and joy before we made this decision. I was able to let go of this man calmly and in full trust of the Lord.

I tell you this story, ladies, because as hard as we may try to battle all of the emotions and thoughts biblically, as diligently as we may apply steps one through five, sometimes God calls us to humble ourselves and take our Boy Box battles to others. I knew in that situation that God was calling me to humble myself. I needed to be prayed over and prayed for. God isn't necessarily calling us to spill all of our struggles and deepest secrets to everyone, but there are times when we need to admit our struggles and boldly ask others to pray for us.

Rewards

What is the positive result when we work at the hard job of keeping the Boy Box under control? There is a song that we sing at our church that comes from Romans 14:17. It goes like this, "Righteousness, peace, joy in the Holy Ghost. Righteousness, peace and joy in the Holy Ghost–that's the kingdom of God." These are our rewards in practicing self-control and trust in God.

1. Righteousness: This word gives me the feeling of being more like Jesus, of basking in the truth and applying it to my life, with the result of looking more like our Lord. When we take our thoughts captive, making them obedient to Christ, we become more like Jesus. We are then able to live in such a way that is more pleasing to God. We are not so consumed with our Boy Box thoughts that we are of no good to anyone else. We can continue to serve him and love him in the midst of the struggle because he will give us what we need to do so. When we are dous-

ing our minds with his Word and living it out, others will benefit as they see the faithfulness of God in our lives.

2. Peace: I hate being anxious. Anxiety is perhaps the latest "craze" to hit our nation. So many people have it and there are anti-anxiety medications to prove it. Jennifer Aniston was Oprah's special guest on today's Oprah show. Since it has now been awhile since Jennifer's divorce from Brad Pitt, Oprah asked her if she was now at peace. Jennifer answered with a confident yes. But peace is not just a feeling we get when our troubles have moved into the distant past. Peace does not have to depend on circumstances or be attainable only when life is less chaotic. The peace that we can receive when having self-control can exist even when we are wrestling, even when nothing has changed in our circumstances, even when there is still a boy attracting our attention and whose attention we so desperately desire to attract. Peace is the confidence we have when we take control of our thoughts and remember whom our trust is in. I like what Paul says in II Timothy 1:12: "That is why I am suffering as I am. Yet I am not ashamed, because I know whom I have believed and am convinced that he is able to guard what I have entrusted to him for that day."

3. Joy: Joy is not just peace and the knowledge that God is in control, but it is a level of happiness that we experience when we see God at work in our lives, when we experience his faithfulness through our suffering. James 1:2–3 boggles my mind each time I read it. "Consider it pure joy, my brothers, whenever you face trials of many kinds, because you know that the testing of your faith develops perseverance." If we embrace our

trials instead of running from them, joy can be a by-product. We can be joyful when we consider how we might become more trusting, persevering children of God. (See more about the battle for joy in chapter seven.)

So, what is it going to be? Will you choose today to take control over your thoughts, including your Boy Box? Do you see a glimmer of hope on the horizon? Do you believe that God can give you righteousness, peace and joy even today? Or will you allow your mind to run freely with thinking that is not pleasing to Him? Will you put false hope in someone who is only human like you and me? Give your mind to the Lord today!

The Single Mom

Have you ever heard the expression "single and free"? This expression brings to mind a happy-go-lucky individual roaming through the world without a burden or care on her shoulders. She comes and goes as she pleases because she doesn't have anyone to report to and she doesn't have anyone reporting to her. Living single and free allows one to live life as she pleases because she does not have a husband or boyfriend to tie her down. But what about those who are single and yet not so free? What about those who need not only for God to be their husbands but also for God to be a full-time father to their children? What about single mothers? (I define a single mother as any woman who is not married, whether divorced, widowed, or never married, and is the main provider for her children.)

Single mother—there is a dichotomy inherent in this much used term. A mother is one who creates children not on her own but with help. A man must be in the picture to create a child. Other than one documented case involving the virgin Mary, a woman *and* a man are always necessary to create a child. There-fore, it seems to follow naturally that a woman and man would be needed to also build a family.

Why then, in our American society, are there more and more families made up of not man, woman and children, but instead only woman and children? A 2002 report from the U.S. Census Bureau[12] shows us that out of all households, 9.2% are run by single moms. (1.9% of households are run by single dads.)

So, nearly 10% of the time it is the woman, the mother, supposedly the weaker partner according to I Peter 3:7, who takes on the role of mother, father, and breadwinner for her family.

The following quotes illustrate the everyday struggles the single mother faces.

"I am a mother, not a father. God created him (the father) to be the head and at times I feel that support missing."

"The hardest thing about being a single mom is being responsible for everything and doing it alone. There is no one to support me or talk things out with who has a real interest in how it all turns out. There is no one to pick up the slack if I can't do it all."

"I struggle when I see other Christian singles that were single with me and now they are married with children and I still haven't had a man show any interest in me—at least not a Christian man."

"It's painful to watch my children growing up in a broken home."

Does our Lord grieve as many women exert tremendous amounts of energy and resources daily just to keep themselves and their families alive? Does our heavenly Father become angry when he witnesses many men leaving their families and shirking their responsibilities? Does Jesus feel pain as the widowed woman with young children struggles to raise them on her own? I believe he does. It is actually amazing to see the many times that God reaches out to the single mom as we read the scriptures. Let us look at a few of these powerful encounters.

Their Hardship–God's Provision

Homeless Hagar–Genesis 16, 21

Hagar is privileged to be employed as the maid of a God-fearing and God-blessed couple. God had promised Abram in Genesis 15 that his offspring would be as many as the stars in the sky. He also told Abram that "a son coming from your own body will be your heir" (Genesis 15:4).

But Abram and Sarai, his wife, get tired of waiting on God to open Sarai's womb. So Sarai devises a plan to have Abram sleep with her maid, Hagar. After Hagar becomes pregnant with Abram's child, her life as she once knew it begins spinning out of control. Just when it becomes most important for her to have security of home and finances, circumstances beyond her control force her out of the only home she has probably ever known.

First, Hagar is forced to flee from Abram and Sarai because of strife and jealousy between the two women. "Then Sarai mistreated Hagar; so she fled from her" (Genesis 16:6b). Hagar has no choice but to leave this abusive situation. However, Hagar leaves this difficult home environment only to find herself with no place to go.

Second, we observe Hagar alone, homeless, deserted and desert-bound when God hears the cries of this single mother-to-be. "For the Lord has heard of your misery" (Genesis 15:11b). Michelle, a single mother of two, recounts, "Sometimes I can only kneel down on the floor of my room and cry out to the Lord for grace to keep going for one more day." The Lord hears Michelle's cries as he heard Hagar's cries on that desperate day.

God then tells Hagar exactly where to go. "Go back to your mistress" (Genesis 16:9a). He also tells Hagar exactly what to do. "Submit to her" (Genesis 16:9b). Let us not miss this. God met Hagar at her point of need. She needed a home. She needed direction. God supplied both. Single mom, what is your need? What is something that must be supplied but can only be supplied by the power of the Lord? Call out to your heavenly Father. Ask him. Expect him to provide. He provided for Hagar. He will provide for you as you trust and obey him. Dwell on this promise. "This is the confidence we have in approaching God: that if we ask anything *according to his will*, he hears us. And if we know that he hears us–whatever we ask–we know that we have what we asked of him" (I John 5:15).

Let us also remember that Hagar ends up homeless a second time when Abraham and Sarah send her packing for good. "Early the next morning Abraham took some food and a skin of water and gave them to Hagar. He set them on her shoulders and then sent her off with the boy" (Genesis 21:14). Again, Hagar finds herself wandering aimlessly through the desert without food, water, or hope for any help. She is even more desperate this time around because she is not alone. She has her young son to provide for. Is God too busy to deal with her in this second crisis situation? No way! Once again, Hagar has needs. She needs food and water and a home. "Then God opened her eyes and she saw a well of water. So she went and filled the skin with water and gave the boy a drink" (Genesis 21:19). If God can provide water in a desert, he can certainly provide for your need. Are you desperate for a place to live? Do you need school clothes for your children? Do you need bus money to get to work? Do you need a job? Cry out to God to meet your need. Remember, God doesn't tire of hearing your cries. You may feel like a broken record asking the Lord for help time and time again, yet God longs for you to depend on him. He desires to be your provider.

The Widow's Wonder Bread–I Kings 17

In between the cities of Tyre and Sidon to the northwest of the Sea of Galilee lived a widow woman and her son. Zarephath was a small town on the Mediterranean Sea. Residents of this quaint beach town probably heard the faint sounds of the sea's repeating waves as they farmed their land and tended to daily chores. For the citizens of this small community, it should have been an ideal place to call home. Unfortunately, the drought in the land had lead to a severe famine. And poor, widowed women were the first to run out of food during those dry times.

This widowed woman probably wondered and worried each day as she looked up and saw not a single cloud in the sky. She used to love waking up to the bright sunshine streaming through her window. But now sunshine meant that she and her son were one day closer to running out of food with no corner store to patronize until the famine ended. Did she pray to the Lord for rain to water the earth? Did she beg God to come to her rescue? We do not know. However, it does appear that she was a God-fearing woman. I Kings 17:12 says, "As surely as the Lord your God lives,' she replied." This statement shows us that she believed wholeheartedly in the Lord. This single woman was a child of God and God enlists help for his child. Elijah, God's prophet, is sent to this desperate daughter to save her and her son from imminent death. God sends this widow a man! (Okay, he is a prophet, not a husband, but he's a godly man that takes care of her—that's pretty cool!)

When Elijah arrives and asks her for bread she responds, "I don't have any bread–only a handful of flour in a jar and a little oil in a jug. I am gathering a few sticks to take home and make a meal for myself and my son, that we may eat it–and die" (I

Kings 17:12b). This woman is in dire straights. She has a visitor, but this visitor is only looking for food just as she is.

Although the widow does not know this, Elijah is from God and has been sent to assist her. He commands her to make a cake of bread for him and then make one for her and her son. And then Elijah promises, "The jar of flour will not be used up and the jug of oil will not run dry until the day the Lord gives rain on the land" (I Kings 17:14b).

"She went away and did as Elijah had told her." This was the widow's step of faith. What does God require of you when you are in need? He requires you to believe. He requires you to do what he tells you to do. Adam Clark[13] describes the monstrous step of faith the widow woman takes:

> "But make me thereof a little cake first"—This was certainly putting the widow's faith to an extraordinary trial: to take and give to a stranger, of whom she knew nothing, the small pittance requisite to keep her child from perishing, was too much to be expected.

And yet the widow obeys. What is God asking you to do? Is he asking you to trust him with your loneliness? Is he asking you to get a job and to trust him to provide childcare? Is he asking you to consult him with each purchase you make so that your spending will glorify him? Is he asking you to trust him to provide money for your child's next dental visit? Pray for your need. Wait on the Lord. Listen to his voice. Step out in obedient faith. He will not leave you stranded. He will provide for the need. He is trustworthy.

A Sorrowful Single Mom–Luke 7

This next woman that God reaches out to lives in a town called Nain. Nain is southwest of the Sea of Galilee where Jesus called his first disciples and later performed many miracles. On this particular day, Jesus makes his way to Nain just in time to witness the funeral procession for a widowed woman's son.

Let's take a moment to put ourselves into the place of this woman. Her husband's life is cut short leaving this mother to care for the needs of her family. Thankfully she has a teenage son who can get work and take care of her and his sisters in their father's place. Suddenly, though, he becomes ill and dies. There is no backup plan to the backup plan. The widow contemplates getting a job, but there is no work to be had for a woman with children in the town of Nain. She wonders how she will farm the land just to put food on the table—that was her son's job. He knew best how to manage the crops. Who will fix the roof when it leaks? Who will protect the family from robbers? Who will take care of her in her old age?

God hears the questions of this widow's heart. *God cares deeply for this woman so he sends his only son on this journey to Nain to raise her only son from the dead.* Like his Father, Jesus is touched when he witnesses the weeping woman. "When the Lord saw her, his heart went out to her and he said, 'Don't cry'" (Luke 7:13). He then raises this only son from the dead and gives him back to his mother.

Again, Jesus is the provider. In this case, he provides a provider for the family. It is amazing to me when you look into God's Word how many times God provides for single moms. It just wasn't feasible for a woman to go out and get a job when there was no longer a husband around. More than once, Jesus provided sons for these women who were on their own (see also II Kings 4:1–7). It is reiterated in story after story in the Bible that God takes care of women, especially the single mom. God is the great provider. God doesn't always provide a husband. Therefore, if you won't settle for anything but a husband, you may be disappointed. Set your heart on God. Look for his provision. Be satisfied with his help. Wait on him. He may provide a husband for you in due season, but until then, he will be your helper, your provider, your lover, your friend, and even a Father to your children. Thank you, Lord!

Real Life Stories of God's Provision

Financial Provision

Roxanne, a long-time friend, shares the following story of God's perfect timing. "Due to my husband's physical abuse, we separated. Four days after he left, I received a back child support check from my son's biological father in the amount of $6,600! I had long since given up on ever receiving this money because he had owed it for over ten years. Little did I know how much I would need that money in the coming months. I didn't know at the time that my marriage would end in divorce and that I would be a single parent again with all the financial responsibility; but God did and He provided for me in an unmistakable way, as if to say, 'Don't worry, I got you covered.'"

Emotional Provision

Kierah, a 29-year-old single mom, has struggled often with those late night times of loneliness. One such night, earlier on in her Christian walk, there was a particularly strong desire to go clubbing. So she went. The boys were left with mom and dad and Kierah felt free to party as long as her desperate heart desired. Neglecting the tug of the Holy Spirit, she was a woman on a mission, not a mission from God, but a mission to fulfill her desires her way. Once there, she quickly looked to purchase some drugs like she would have in the old days. She made her move and approached a girl who she knew could get her whatever she wanted. But Kierah did not escape from the Lord that night. He followed her to this "den of iniquity." When Kierah went to make her purchase, the girl refused to sell the "items" to her. For whatever reason, this drug dealer who was out to make as much money as she could that night, would not sell any drugs to Kierah. Kierah remembers that event as a defining moment in her walk with the Lord. She experienced firsthand his protective shield even in the midst of her worldly wanderings.

Kierah continues to experience occasional times of loneliness. She sometimes aches for the Lord to give her a husband to help her with the task of raising two boys and to fulfill her own physical desires. However, she has learned that visiting a club or engaging in a one-night stand will only lead to more heartache. During those times of temptation, she has learned to bring to mind all of the consequences that would probably befall her if she were to give in to the flesh. Those consequences might include: portraying a terrible example to her two young boys, experiencing the pain of rejection from a man she was once intimate with, or catching a disease. Most of all, she fears separating herself from the lover of her soul, Jesus, because of her rebellion.

Instead of looking to the world to solve her moments of crises, she cries out to the Lord with her struggles, "Lord, I'm lonely!" "I long for the touch of a man!" "How long will I be alone?" She has known the comfort of her heavenly Father during those times as she calls out to him in complete honesty and senses his listening ear and caring heart. She still does not know if or when the Lord will bring that person into her life, but God has provided for her in so many ways, including the provision of his gentle, healing hand in times of emotional pain. Kierah trusts God as each emotional need arises. She knows now that she will come out of emotional turmoil understanding even more deeply God's love and faithfulness.

Father-figure Provision

One of the single ladies I spoke with had a deep desire for her boys, ages twelve and six, to have the influence of Christian men in their lives. She felt such a burden for this that she began to pray consistently for God to bring some men to reach out to her kids. She went before the throne of grace with confidence to find mercy and grace to help her in her time of need (see Hebrews 4:16). Let this be an encouragement to you, single mother, to bring before the Lord your needs and the needs of your children. God doesn't demand a perfect prayer warrior. He simply beckons you to lay your requests before him with a heart of humility and the faith of a mustard seed.

It wasn't too long after these prayers were prayed that God laid it on the heart of a godly man in the church (with young kids of his own, by the way) to reach out to her oldest son. For several months he spent time with this boy going through Bible study materials and just hanging out. To this day, she is pleased to say that she can list four or five men in her church that reach out to her boys on a regular basis. It may just be to chat or play with them after church or at a social gathering. But it has meant that godly male influences have been a consistent part of their lives ever since the first prayers for God to move in this area were uttered. God is a great provider!

The single mother has deep needs, as we all do, that are compounded by raising children alone. I urge those of you who are single without children to pray for the Lord to place a single mom in your path to befriend. You may be able to take her kids on an outing while their mom catches up on some much-needed rest or quiet time with the Lord. You may be able to accompany her on errands so that she has an adult to talk with for a few hours. You may be able to invite this mom and her children to your house for dinner and board games. Take a moment now to consider with whom the Lord is calling you to take initiative.

Lord, I pray for those single moms who are reading this book that they may be encouraged to trust more deeply in you as they seek your face and watch you work on their behalf. Amen.

I'll never forget my sixth grade year in school. It was 1978 and I had finally obtained 12-year-old status. I had good grades and a few good friends. I had moved up the ranks to become Eaton Elementary School's tetherball champion. I even carried a Donny and Marie Show lunch box. It seemed that nothing could go wrong in such a blessed life. But something certainly did go wrong over the course of that year. Slowly but surely the kids at school began to avoid me like the plague. The demise of my social life became apparent as I overheard a group of friends plotting against me in the girl's bathroom. They didn't know I was in one of the stalls, and so the cutting words were heard by me unbeknownst to those little gossipers. They shattered my sixth grade world with statements like, "I don't like Jane anymore." "Don't tell Jane what we're talking about." "She's not really part of our group." I realized at that moment that these so-called friends no longer wanted me around. The rest of that year, I felt lonelier than I had ever felt in my short life.

As you have probably also experienced in life, some people just do not like us and do not want us around. Some people reject us and whether we are 14 or 40, it is painful. Fortunately, God never rejects us. He may be displeased with us, but he never wants us to go away. As a matter of fact, he actually insists that we remain close to him at all times.

John 15:5 says, "I am the vine and you are the branches. If a man remains in me and I in him, he will bear much fruit. Apart from me, you can do nothing." This is the Christian's biggest challenge—to walk closely with Christ, obeying his Word and the promptings of the Holy Spirit. And yet God doesn't expect anything less. Yes indeed, he is a jealous God. He loves us beyond what we have ever experienced love to be. And for that I can only say thank you to the only one who runs after me, never rejecting me, but desiring fellowship with me every moment of my life.

Frances J. Roberts in his book *Come Away My Beloved*[14] expresses beautifully the Father's love for us, his children.

O My beloved, abide under the shelter of the lattice–for I have betrothed thee unto Myself, and though ye are sometimes indifferent toward Me, My love for thee is at all times as a flame of fire. My ardor never cools. My longing for thy love and affection is deep and constant.

Psalm 103:11 says, "For as high as the heavens are above the earth, so great is his love for those who fear him."

God saddens when friends, family, hobbies, problems, and just general busyness get between us and him. So with his still, small and yet nagging voice, his Holy Spirit, he calls. He calls to us during the day when we are at work and we forget to acknowledge him. He calls when we allow temptations of the world to draw us away from him, even for a second. He calls when we are crying tears of loneliness and desperation and feel like the world holds no hope for us. He calls at every twist and turn in our lives. *Never does he wish for this cord of fellowship to be broken.*

I am reminded of a passage in my favorite book by Charlotte Bronte, *Jane Eyre*[15]. In it Mr. Rochester, a wealthy, educated man expresses his love to Jane, the poor, plain nanny of his daughter Adele:

> "Because," he said, "I sometimes have a queer feeling with regard to you–especially when you are near me, as now: it is as if I had a string somewhere under my left ribs, tightly and inextricably knotted to a similar string situated in the corresponding quarter of your little frame. And if that boisterous Channel, and two hundred miles or so of land come broad between us, I am afraid that cord of communion will be snapt; and then I've a nervous notion I should take to bleeding inwardly."

Mr. Rochester loved this girl even though she owned nothing. She did not possess wealth, status, family, or fame to offer him in return. She could only give to him herself and her love. After he desperately pleads with Jane to become his wife, she returns his love and accepts his offer of marriage.

Like Mr. Rochester and Jane, there is something like an invisible cord that connects us to the one who so desperately loves us. Unlike Mr. Rochester's cord of communion, however, neither distance, time, sin, nor rebellion will ever break the cord that binds us to the lover of our souls. *We are bound forever and, as each day passes, that cord is reeled in closer and closer to the heart of God.* Daily he pulls. Daily he whispers his love to us. Daily he reminds us that we are his.

Feeling Full

Not only does God persistently pursue us, but he also promises that when we yield to his advances, we will be filled to all fullness. The following verses promise us satisfaction in him.

> John 10:10: "The thief comes only to steal and kill and destroy; I have come that they may have life and have it to the full."
>
> Psalm 16:11: "You will make known to me the path of life; In your presence is fullness of joy; In Your right hand there are pleasures forever." (NAS)

So this brings us to some deep questions that you may be asking. *"Why don't I feel complete with just me and the Lord? Why do I feel like something is missing?"* Lord, we desire to know what you meant when you said "in your presence is fullness of joy." I don't claim to be a theologian, but I am a follower of Christ and, therefore, a student of the Word. Let us talk together about what it may mean, single sister, to find fullness in and through Jesus.

First, take a moment to try and absorb the meanings of the words full and joy.

The Random House Dictionary[16] offers these definitions:

- joy: 1. the emotion of great delight or happiness caused by something good or satisfying 2. a source of keen pleasure or delight
- full: 1. filled to utmost capacity 2. complete or entire 3. of the maximum amount, extent etc. 4. abundant or well-supplied

Barnes makes the following comment concerning John

10:10: "The word (full) denotes that which is not absolutely essential to life, but which is superadded to make life happy. They shall not merely have life—simple, bare existence—but they shall have all those superadded things which are needful to make that life eminently blessed and happy."[17]

In addition, I did a little Greek study on the word translated full in the NIV. The Greek word perisson *does* mean full, or abundant. The word connotes the idea of being complete or lacking nothing. The NAS version of the Bible translates John 10:10 this way, "I came that they may have life and have it abundantly." I like the Random House Dictionary [18] definition of abundant: "richly supplied."

I just finished a personal-sized Round Table pineapple and mushroom pizza. While visiting family in California, I purposely set aside one or two meals to enjoy this pizza that, in my opinion, is tastier than even Chicago-style pizza. From the soft and crispy crust to the perfect blend of cheeses and tomato sauce to the fresh (not canned) mushrooms, I definitely feel full and satisfied after my rendezvous with this culinary delight! What food fills your belly to a satisfying swell? Is it your mom's home-cooked meatloaf? Is it New York Super Fudge Chunk ice cream from Ben and Jerry's? Or is it steak and potatoes from your favorite chophouse? (Okay, take a break, go get a bowl of ice cream and come back—come on, this isn't a diet book!) Whatever your filling food of choice, we all know it is often easier to satisfy the demands of our growling bellies—our physical appetites—than it is to satisfy the hunger of our souls.

But what of emotional and spiritual fullness that is promised to us in these scriptures? Is this also a satisfying swelling of yet a different organ? Should my heart feel so full, satisfied and contented that life itself becomes a completely wonderful experience? Do I have a right to expect 24/7 satisfaction?

I believe that God does desire for us to get to a point of fullness in him—where even our emotions and circumstances don't chase away our joy and fullness of life. However, this is hard work. What does fullness truly look like? I sense we need to break down this illusive concept a bit more that we may know what the promises and rewards are of seeking after him.

What does every human being on this planet long for? We long for relationships with other people. We also long for unconditional acceptance and love in those relationships. We were made for that very thing—to be in relationship with God and with each other. If we are no longer craving that, it is simply because we have been hurt by others. We have allowed our tender, beating heart to become cold, hard and closed to loving and caring for others.

God is always pursuing us to have constant relationship with him. When we respond to that pursuit by walking and talking with him, we come to know him more. Our spirits come alive and our souls actually connect with the God who created us. No longer does life only consist of working and eating and daily chores and weddings and funerals and striving to stay alive while planning out our own destinies. Instead, life becomes an adventure. God's perfect plan begins to take shape. Each day becomes one of learning more about him and taking steps of faith. Even amidst problems and times of grief, there is the joy of knowing that God is going to do a new thing! Ultimately, life becomes full of love and meaning and purpose and direction. This is where fullness comes to fruition—in the day-by-day, moment-by-moment trusting and walking with Jesus as he walked with his Father. This abundant life and overflowing joy is possible. Jesus came for this very thing. But...

Our Daily Battle

Psalm 1:2–3 says, "But his delight is in the law of the Lord, and on his law he meditates day and night. He is like a tree planted by streams of water, which yields its fruit in season and whose leaf does not wither. Whatever he does prospers."

As hard as God consistently tries to get hold of our hearts, we must also work to maintain our connection with him. This is where we are able to find fullness, when we fight hard to hold his hand and walk with him through every up and down along the road of life.

Even in the midst of struggles with loneliness and discontentment, we can prosper if we decide to renew our minds with his Word. However, this is often difficult as circumstances and emotions bombard us with arrows that penetrate to the core of our beings. For example, loneliness can be so overwhelming that God doesn't seem to be enough to shoulder the burden. Sin's short-term pleasures sometimes seem worth the consequences when we feel so down-and-out, especially when obedience isn't bringing that immediate feel-good experience.

Fortunately, there are some characters from biblical history who were in highly difficult circumstances but still remained faithful to the Lord and even came out on the other side victorious. They may not have had consistent feelings of happiness and joy in the midst of the fiery trials, but they strove to trust in God as circumstances became what most would consider unbearable.

Job

One evening after a long day of work, I came home, threw my hair into a pony tail, put on my pajamas, and bundled into my blue fleece robe. Next, I began preparing a delectable gourmet meal of frozen fish filets and French fries. While they were cooking slowly on a cookie sheet in the oven, I opened my cupboard to pull down my Heinz ketchup. Unfortunately, to my utter dismay, the bottle was nearly empty. There was certainly not enough to complement the frozen food.

My mind began to reel as my stomach growled with intense need. At that moment, the thought of fish and fries with no ketchup was not a solution—but the timer was ticking. With no time to spare, I grabbed $2.00, tied on my gym shoes, and replaced my robe with a light-weight jacket. I sprinted across the busy street near my house—in my pajamas—to a small pantry. Sure enough, there was a bottle of no-name ketchup perched on the shelf. I debated about purchasing it but knew I could not settle for anything but Heinz. So, I ran. I ran down the street and around the corner as fast as I could, hoping that no one would notice that I was out and about in my nightwear. I knew as I approached Walgreen's that it was my last hope so I dashed into the store and down the food aisle. I was pleasantly surprised to find the Heinz bottle waiting for my arrival. I looked at the price and, *oh no,* it was $2.00 before the tax. I quickly calculated and realized I was a few cents short, but I took a risk and went to the checkout. Completely out of breath I explained my predicament. Fortunately, the clerk was gracious to take my $2 and forego the four cents I still owed him. I sprinted back to my house as dusk was settling in, knowing that this dinner would be just as good as I had originally imagined—Heinz ketchup included!

Some things in life take added determination—that "I will not give up no matter what" attitude. Job was one who had that attitude. He determined in his mind to never give up on trusting the Lord—no matter what.

Let us keep in mind that the promise Jesus makes in John 10:10 had not been made yet. However, Job "was blameless and upright; he feared God and shunned evil." God had revealed himself to Job even though Job lived before Moses and, therefore, did not have the benefit of the written Word of God. So when God allows Satan to bring terrible suffering on this man of God, including death and destruction of all he knew and loved, Job remains faithful and does not curse God.

Job is honest, however, in the way that he speaks to God. In Chapter 30, he does not hesitate to express how he feels distant and even attacked by the Lord.

"I cry out to you, O God, but you do not answer; I stand up, but you merely look at me. You turn on me ruthlessly; with the might of your hand you attack me. You snatch me up and drive me before the wind; you toss me about in the storm." (v. 22)

"The churning inside me never stops; days of suffering confront me." (v. 27)

Maintaining a connection with God does not always mean that we will feel better instantaneously. Job continued to trust in the Lord through his horrific ordeal, but he suffered intensely while continuing to rely on the Master.

The incredible thing about Job is that although he felt that God was against him and that he was even causing his suffering, he did not use this as an excuse to sin.

Job 30:31 says, "My harp is tuned to mourning, and my flute to the sound of wailing." He is an utterly distressed and destitute man. But what does he say next in Job 31:1? "I made a covenant with my eyes not to look lustfully at a girl."

Job is definitely in the depths of despair but he doesn't allow his feelings to control his actions. He continues to walk uprightly through emotional and physical pain that we will probably never experience.

Through this traumatic trial did Job continue to have joy? Remember what David said, "In your presence is fullness of joy." Remember, Job did not have the benefit of the Holy Spirit living inside of him. Just like many righteous men in the Old Testament, he relied on God to communicate with him directly. Because God does not initiate with Job, Job does not have the presence of the Lord throughout much of his ordeal. So Job must rely on what he knows of God from the past. Job definitely did not have consistent joy. This is apparent in Job 3:3: "May the day of my birth perish and the night it was said, 'A boy is born!'" Job wished he was never born. Have you ever wished you were never born? Has your loneliness or sadness or hurt been so overwhelming that motivation to keep living is scarce?

Job found that God was still enough in the midst of deep despair and trial. Job 13:15 says, "Though he slay me, yet will I hope in him." Job's mind was made up. No matter what would and could befall him, he would trust in God. Has God proved himself trustworthy in your life? Have you seen his faithfulness in the past? Then when hard times hit, when despair lingers, when sadness boils over to hopelessness, when singleness is beyond what you can bear, trust in him. We have no other choice once we have tasted that the Lord is good. We must cling to him. *We must not use our misery as an opportunity to sin.* We must remain steadfast and by all means, as Paul exhorts us in Ephesians 6:13, "put on the full armor of God, so that when the day of evil comes, you may be able to stand your ground, and after you have done everything, to stand."

As we can see in Job's life, finding fullness in God does not always mean we will feel happy and contented, but it does mean that we have found that God is enough.

Psalm 30:5 says, "weeping may remain for a night, but rejoicing comes in the morning." There will be times of deep suffering in the life of the Christian. But God does promise us fullness and joy in his presence. It may not be constant, but it will come as we trust in him. That is the great promise. The alternative is to attempt to satiate your desires with the temporary happiness of the world. But God commands us not to do this. "Do not love the world or anything in the world… the world and its desires pass away, but the man who does the will of God lives forever" (I John 2:15, 17).

This doesn't mean that we as believers don't have these desires to have a great time! And I don't mean "potluck at the church" kind of good time. Today is December 20. The last few days I have been plotting in my mind how I can make this New Year's Eve a night to remember. I've been trying to figure out how I can obtain some guy to be my date for the night. Is there someone at church that would go "as a friend"? Or perhaps there is a way I could rent a date. Maybe I'd even have an opportunity to witness to him during the night on the town!

Going somewhere with a guy friend or renting a date may or may not be wrong (okay, I was really kind of joking about the rent-a-date thing—don't do it!) but where is my focus as I plot and plan for a super special evening? Is it to find temporary happiness? Honestly, yes. After all, didn't someone once say, "Girls just want to have fun"? Jesus did everything for the glory of the Father. So I ask myself even now, "what would glorify God on New Year's Eve?" Wow, this helps get my eyes off of me, myself and I and onto serving Christ even on that special night. It makes me think—who can I minister to? Can I have people over who have nowhere to go, perhaps other singles? Can I deliver food and tracts to those without food and shelter?

Several years ago, on Christmas day, my friend Eileen and I found ourselves far away from family. She longed for a room full of brothers, sisters, nieces and nephews. I longed for my mom's homemade turkey and stuffing. As we thought of our loved ones while eating a less than typical holiday meal, we remembered the nursing home in our neighborhood. We thought of the many people in that place who would pass through another Christmas without a single visit. So we walked over to the home and sat with several older people. We listened. We talked. We gave hugs. We shared Jesus. What could have been another half-baked holiday became one of the best holidays I have ever experienced as an adult. Times of loneliness and longing can become times of blessing and fullness. Lord, when our eyes are so fixed on fulfilling our own desires, help us to instead look to you for your answers to our longings. Amen.

David

David was the one who said it—he is the one who has created in us this notion in our minds that knowing God would bring happiness. In Psalm 16:11 David says, "You will make known to me the path of life. In your presence is fullness of joy."

And yet we witness David more than any other Bible character, on so many occasions, nearly drowning in the depths of sorrow. Can despair and joy co-exist? Can we know the joy of the Lord and yet not feel the joy of the Lord? Why did David talk about God's presence bringing joy when it is apparent through some of his writings that he is beaten down and discouraged, even *in* God's presence?

David's writings in the psalms do reveal to us how joy and sorrow can walk together—almost hand in hand. In the following psalms, we observe David living through times of emotional distress and yet clinging to God. We witness David experiencing joy in the midst of turmoil because of his unwavering belief in God's faithfulness. Let us look at how, in each of the following psalms, David is in the pit, yet is able to think of and sometimes even know joy.

Psalm 27: In verses 2–3 of this psalm, David speaks of his enemies attacking him and evil men advancing against him. Even in these terrifying circumstances, David thinks of joy. Verse six says, "… at his tabernacle will I sacrifice with shouts of joy; I will sing and make music to the Lord." And in verse 14, "Wait for the Lord; be strong and take heart and wait for the Lord." David may not have fully felt joy at those moments of trial, but his knowledge of God's deliverance and promises drove him to be able to consider joy and fully believe he would actually experience it once again.

Psalm 42: In this psalm, David is remembering the joy that he used to have. Verse 4: "how I used to go with the multitude leading the procession to the house of God with shouts of joy and thanksgiving…" Do you sometimes wonder—where did my joy go? Just last week I had such an ache of loneliness and, in addition, a discouraging time in my ministry that I could not even imagine being joyful again. However, I remembered how God had been my joy in the past. I remembered the many times he had lifted *me* from the pit. So even in despair, I was not hopeless, because I remembered. Are you remembering what God has done for you in the past? Are you trusting God to revive you once again as he has done before? If you have never experienced his mighty right arm lifting you from the ash heap, I can only tell you it is because you have wallowed so much in your despair that you have not allowed him to lift you. Test him and try him this time. He will show himself faithful and begin the inner-workings of joy in your heart. In verse 5 David expresses the depth of his struggle. "Why are you downcast, O my soul? Why so disturbed within me? Put your hope in God, for I will yet praise him, my Savior and my God." Despair and joy may not co-exist at exactly the same moment, but hope in God can exist with despair. When we hope in him and he shows himself trustworthy, joy follows rather quickly. Our next psalm, Psalm 30, demonstrates this truth.

Psalm 30: Verse three says, "O Lord, you brought me up from the grave; you spared me from going down into the pit." And verse five reminds us that, "weeping may remain for a night, but rejoicing comes in the morning." Finally, verse 11 states, "You turned my wailing into dancing; you removed my sackcloth and clothed me with joy." God does not want us to stay miserable forever. He knows we can only take so much. Yes, sometimes it seems we are at the end of our rope. However, what happens when you are dangling in midair at the end of a rope with nothing to catch your fall if you let go? You cling tighter to the rope to avoid your sudden death! The struggle of singleness can be so hard at times that you will feel like you want to let go of the rope (Jesus) and give up. You get tired of clinging to him. The enemy tempts and taunts you to try his way—to look to the world to get what you want. At that point, you must remember what is true. If I let go of the rope (Jesus), I will surely die. There is no other option in your struggle than to keep your hands firmly clutching onto your Savior. After all, there is a promise—"joy WILL come in the morning." Thank you, Father, that even though you don't have to lift us out of the mud and mire, you do, because of your great love for us!

You may not be feeling joy at the moment, but is there the hope of joy? For me there is some kind of a joy or comfort in the hope of joy. When I am in mortal agony, I have learned to trust in God just enough to put one foot in front of the other. I remember that joy will come in the morning. If we have nothing else to hope in, at the very least we have the hope of eternal life. Remember—joy is born out of hope. Just remember to hope in the right thing—in him who is able to keep you from falling! He is our fullness!

Conclusion

I rarely read the conclusions in books and I know you're tired, so I'll keep this short. Single sister—are you called to singleness today? Walk heartily with God through this single season of life. Turn from the temptation to settle for second best. Keep your eyes fixed on the eternal gift of grace. Take every thought captive. And, lastly, thank God for the benefits and blessings you have been given during these days, months or years of singleness. Girlfriend, work that singleness for the glory of God!

Top Ten Challenges of Living Single

1. Going to weddings alone… but dancing with anyone you want!
2. Coming home to an empty house… with only your mess to clean up!
3. No backrubs… to give!
4. Waiting for Mr. Right… but at least you didn't settle for Mr. Wrong!
5. Cooking for one… and cleaning dirty dishes for one!
6. Becoming more selfish… but having freedom to consider your dreams!
7. Getting all-consuming crushes on guys… but— no, this is just bad.

8. Feeling misunderstood by married people… but being loved and cared for by some of them!

9. Sitting alone in church… but meeting new people around you!

And number ten.…

10. No guarantee to have a companion for the holidays… but no cranky in-laws to deal with!

Okay, I just thought you might want to get that little whining session out of the way. Now here's the good stuff!

Top 20 Benefits of Living Single

1. Eating whenever you want
2. Eating wherever you want—living room, bedroom etc.
3. Listening to whatever music you want in the car
4. Setting the thermostat in the house and car to your perfect temperature
5. If living alone, having people over whenever you want
6. Consulting only God on where to spend your money
7. Going out to dinner with friends whenever the mood hits
8. Going ice skating while other moms your age are trying to tie skates on to their screaming kids!
9. Playing the sports and games at the church retreat while other women your age are running after their kids
10. Laying in bed when you're sick instead of taking care of your husband and kids who may also feel yucky

11. Renting a "chick flick" and not getting in trouble for it
12. Making macaroni and cheese for dinner and no one complains
13. Spending every Christmas with your side of the family
14. Participating in last-minute ministry opportunities without consulting anyone
15. Going through the drive thru at McDonald's and not paying $20 (as you would if you had a family)
16. Going on vacation to wherever you want
17. Going on a mission trip at any time
18. Ordering pizza with only veggies—no meat
19. Becoming a contestant on Survivor, Amazing Race, etc. without worrying about leaving your family for 40 days

And number twenty...

20. You can still continue to dream about the wonderful guy that the Lord might have for you right around the corner!

God's Plan

- God created people. Genesis 1:27
- God told them they could eat from any tree in the garden, but one. Genesis 2:16–17
- The people disobeyed God and ate from the forbidden tree. Genesis 3
- Since that time, all people have been born sinners. Romans 5:12
- God said that sin must be paid for by the shedding of blood. Hebrews 9:22
- So God became flesh and walked on the earth. While he was here, he showed us how to live. See Matthew, Mark, Luke, John. Jesus also shed

his blood for us in death, dying on a cross to pay the penalty for our sin. I John 2:2. He also rose from the dead—conquering death for those who would believe in him. Matthew 28:7

- Why did God do this? Because he loves his creation and desires relationship with us. He wants us to know his love as a good father loves his child. Romans 5:8
- How do you begin in a relationship with God? Repent and believe in Jesus. Acts 17:30–31
- Romans 10:9: "That if you confess with your mouth 'Jesus is Lord,' and believe in your heart God raised him from the dead, you will be saved." See also John 5:24, I John 4:7–8
- Ask God to lead you to a Bible teaching church so you might grow in your relationship with the God of the universe!

Endnotes

1   Emma Thompson *Sense and Sensibility* (Columbia Pictures 1995)

2   James Blunt "You're Beautiful" *Back to Bedlam* Atlantic, 2005.

3   Weird Al Yankovic "You're Pitiful," 2006.

4   Biblical Counseling Center of Arlington Heights

5   Josh Groban "You Raise Me Up" *Closer* Reprise, 2003.

6   Edith Wharton, *Ethan Frome* (New York: New American Library, 2000)

7   Bill Thrasher, *Believing God for His Best* (Chicago: Moody, 2004), 35–36

8   Gary Chapman, *The Five Love Languages* (Chicago: Northfield Publishing, 1992)

9   Frances J. Roberts, *Come Away My Beloved* (Ojai, California: King's Farspan, Inc., 1973), p. 110

10   J.K. Rowling, *Harry Potter and the Goblet of Fire* (Arthur A. Levine Books: New York, 2000)

11   *Harry Potter and the Goblet of Fire*, p. 597

12   The U.S. Census Bureau, 2002, http://www.census.gov/Press-Release/www/2003/cb03–97.html

13   Adam Clark's Commentary on the Old Testament Electronic Edition STEP Files Copyright © 1999, Parsons Technology, Inc., all rights reserved.

14   Frances J. Roberts, *Come Away My Beloved* (Ojai, California: King's Farspan, Inc., 1973), 13

15   Charlotte Bronte, *Jane Eyre,* (Naples, Florida: Trident Press International, 2001), 241

16   Stuart Berg Flexner, Editor in Chief, *The Random House Dictionary*, (New York: Random House, 1978) 356, 479

17   *Barnes' Notes on the New Testament* Electronic Edition STEP Files Copyright © 1999, Findex.Com. All rights reserved.

18   Stuart Berg Flexner, Editor in Chief, *The Random House Dictionary*, (New York: Random House, 1978), 4

TATE PUBLISHING & *Enterprises*

Tate Publishing is committed to excellence in the publishing industry. Our staff of highly trained professionals, including editors, graphic designers, and marketing personnel, work together to produce the very finest books available. The company reflects the philosophy established by the founders, based on Psalms 68:11,

"THE LORD GAVE THE WORD AND GREAT WAS THE COMPANY OF THOSE WHO PUBLISHED IT."

If you would like further information, please call
1.888.361.9473
or visit our website
www.tatepublishing.com

TATE PUBLISHING & *Enterprises*, LLC
127 E. Trade Center Terrace
Mustang, Oklahoma 73064 USA